LIVING
ABOVE YOUR
CIRCUMSTANCES

—————

Stories of Courageous
Overcoming

DIANE E. HUNTER

ENDORSEMENTS

"No matter what you're facing in life, the dynamic principles in *Living Above Your Circumstances* will speak directly to your heart. The stories shared in this book will help you successfully walk out your own life's story.

Diane writes from a personal, intimate knowledge of what it means to love a merciful God in the midst of difficult circumstances."

—Dr. Andrew Bills,
Apostle and Founder of Holy Spirit Broadcasting Network

"Diane Hunter has a unique perspective from her experience and faith walk. What she's learned transcends the natural and resides in a place called hope.

Living Above Your Circumstances is an example of how the Lord can use the difficulties others have experienced to speak to the dry and rocky places in our own lives.

I highly recommend this book for anyone who is having a difficult time navigating trials and the situations that are overwhelming and confounding in their daily walk with the Lord."

—Dr. Carol Dickey,
International Speaker and Singer

"In a world where people turn to the Internet for immediate answers, Diane Hunter makes the case for the spiritual value of not always having an immediate answer. She provides profound and powerful insight into the types of questions that Google and social media will never be able to answer. In doing so she attempts to prevent the disillusionment caused by not turning to God and receiving His unconditional love."

—Scott Paladichuk,
Community Leader and Minister, Orange County

"*Living Above Your Circumstances* touches on the deep subject of what to do when disappointments and questions come in our walk with God. Diane Hunter's book shows us the importance of seeking God and His Word as we find "peace in the midst of the storm." She beautifully shows how God is our lifeline as she shares from her own experience how to walk out these principles. Diane is an amazing example of a gracious woman of faith!

This book would be valuable in your personal library as well as a source of study material for small groups."

—Heidi Alvarado,
Worship Leader at Vineyard at the River

"I cannot think of a more qualified person to write *Living Above Your Circumstances* than my friend, Diane Hunter. I honestly believe that it is a must-read for everyone. We will all have moments of disappointment, despair, and confusion in our faith journeys. It is natural to question our faith in God and His promises in challenging times. This is not wrong to do. The difficulty actually arises when we do not voice these questions for fear of rebuke, judgment, and shame.

This book walks through these valleys and invites God into the midst of them—interweaving Scripture and powerful stories that will draw you in and through to the other side... to a place of freedom!"

—Pastor Patti Helzer,
Mourning to Morning Ministries

"I am delighted to recommend Diane Hunter's new book, *Living Above Your Circumstances*. As I read I was reminded of the beautiful and powerful truths in God's Word, and was pulled deeper into the Father's heart.

Diane's vulnerability and transparency is riveting as she describes testimonies of what supernatural courage looks like. Because God has helped her to overcome and has given her His eternal perspective, she has laid a solid foundation for others to walk victoriously above their circumstances. "

—Vicki Lund,
Pastor, Broadcaster, and Co-Founder of Joy in Christ Ministries

©copyright 2020 Roger & Diane Hunter, Epic Life Ministries
www.epiclifeministries.com

ISBN13: 978-0-578-62579-9

Published by Epic Life Ministries

Versions of Bible Translation:
ESV—English Standard Version
NASB—New American Standard Bible
NHEB—New Heart English Bible
NIV—New International Version
NKJV—New King James Version
NLT—New Living Translation
TLB—Translation, Living Bible
TPT—The Passion Translation

Writing Perspectives:
• I capitalize God pronouns in the text and in all Bible verses.
• I use the all capital "LORD" in Scripture verses—this stands for
  YHWH, which is how the Jewish people wrote Yahweh.

DEDICATION

~ To all who have been seeking answers—
who continue to stand when life doesn't make sense.

~ To my precious friends who have walked through
profoundly challenging circumstances—
Deborah Darone
Elizabeth Benkovich
Jill Bougher
Sara Dennis
It's been an honor to journey with you
as we find our victory.

~ To Coleen Garcia,
my role model—
who finished her race well.
Having endured so much
she's now part of the great cloud of witnesses,
enjoying the eternal reward of her overcoming.
Coleen, the testimony of your life is engraved in my heart.
Thanks for praying into and prophesying over this book.
I love you and miss you!

ACKNOWLEDGMENTS

Rick Adams—
Thank you for your feedback in clarifying content while this book was still a work in progress. The questions you posed and the conversations you prompted were invaluable in bringing it to completion.

Elizabeth Benkovich—
Thank you for your insight and ability to help me clearly articulate my writing. You are brilliant at seeing past the surface of the words to the heart of what I wanted to say. I so value your perspective.

Caitlin Scudder Guess—
Thank you for your skilled editing—especially in correcting my grammar. You are truly gifted, and I am grateful for how you have helped the book flow. Your willingness, excellence, and proficiency, in doing this touched my heart deeply.

Gary & Teri Stache—
Thank you for your generous contribution in helping to fund the publishing of this book. We are truly overwhelmed for how you've sown into this project, and are so grateful for how you model sharing God's heart of truth and mercy to the world around you.

Mike Youngsma—
Thank you for using your creativity in designing the book's cover and for beautifully formatting the layout. I appreciate you and am grateful for your partnering with me to get it published.

FOREWORD

When you look for a description of a literary foreword you will see that it is typically written by a famous or noteworthy person in the field of the book topic. Although I have a Master of Arts degree in Marriage and Family Ministries, what makes me noteworthy is the position I hold, that no one else in the world has: I have been best friends with the author of this book for over 25 years. Because of this I am uniquely qualified to share with you who she is and why this book is so meaningful.

From the time I met Diane at Talbot School of Theology in 1993 it was apparent that she had a particularly genuine and personal relationship with Jesus. Year after year since then I have watched her relationship with Him continue to deepen, expand, and mature.

I have had a front row seat to her real life, seeing her celebrate triumphs as well as struggle with disappointments and great pain. Through it all she has only gained more intimacy and understanding of God and His ways. Her life has proven to me again and again that you can not only hold on but truly live as a powerful, real Christian through great hardship and suffering. She is a diamond. It is so good that she has written this book identifying and explaining ways to overcome through very difficult times. She knows of what she speaks.

It is clear to me that God has inspired Diane to write this book in order to share with you practical yet prismatic ways to work through this life—especially when you may feel you don't know what to think or do to keep going with Him. It has been through devotion, prayer, study, pain, and the Holy Spirit, that these keys have been tested into Diane's being and are now being shared in this book. I pray that as you walk through these pages you receive insights, hope, and love from God that are uniquely personal.

Elizabeth Benkovich, M.A. in Marriage & Family Ministries,
Talbot School of Theology, November 2019

"Behold, the eye of the LORD is on those who fear Him,
on those who **hope in His mercy…**
Let Your mercy, O LORD,
be upon us,
just as we hope in You."

Psalm 33:22; NKJV, bold added

CONTENTS

INTRODUCTION

Have you ever hoped or believed for something with all of your heart and it didn't happen? How did that affect you?

- Did it sow doubt and disappointment in your heart?
- Did you become disillusioned?
- Did it change how you related to God?
- Or were you able to find God's perspective in it?

At some point in your life, you will be at these crossroads. You will pray and believe for something that doesn't work out the way you wanted. If you understand that this is a necessary part of life—and there is purpose in it—you will prosper and overcome instead of losing heart.

Living Above Your Circumstances looks at real-to-life scenarios that show you how you can overcome when:

- your circumstances are difficult;
- an area of your life doesn't make sense;
- your deepest desires are unfulfilled.

As you journey through this book, I invite you to ask the hard questions. Allow the Lord into those deep places. He is there. He is in the questions, the disappointments, the not understanding. As you seek, you will find your answers. There *are* answers.[1] But more importantly, you will find Him—in the glitches, misunderstandings, and even the heartbreaks of your life.

There are treasures here. God has hidden gems in the difficulties that you're facing. *Living Above Your Circumstances* looks at how unanswered prayers and deferred dreams can either dishearten you or equip you for greatness. We will dig deep, searching out what God has to say. And we will find His heart, restoration, and perspective here.

> "'And I will give you treasures hidden in the darkness—
> secret riches.
> I will do this so you may know that I am the LORD,
> the God of Israel, the One who calls you by name.
> 'And why have I called you for this work?
> Why did I call you by name when you did not know Me?
> ...I have equipped you for battle...
> ...so all the world from east to west will know...
> I am the LORD, and there is no other.'" Isaiah 45:3-4a, 5b, 6;
> NLT

If something is difficult and doesn't make sense, seek Him. Ask God what He is doing in you, in it.
- What are His Kingdom purposes for you?
- Is God using it to strengthen and mature you?
- Or is it an attack from the enemy that you are supposed to stand against and take dominion over?

---

[1] You may not get a specific answer as to why you lost your child... spouse... job, or home... But as you seek Him, He will give you the clarity you need to bring you hope and freedom again.

My prayer is that as you read this book you will be encouraged by the courageous ones who have shared their stories. May you be inspired to step into your own breakthroughs as you consider how they have overcome.

Each chapter is comprised of:
1. An introduction of that chapter's topic;
2. Someone's overcoming story;
3. Scripture interwoven with the content;
4. A "Key to Victory";
5. A "Message from God's Heart."

The last section of each chapter, "Message from God's Heart," is what I felt God wanted to say to encourage you personally. It's amazing how He can speak to each of us[2] even though we all have different life circumstances. I pray these messages will draw you more deeply into His heart so you can receive the fullness of His love for you.

---

[2] Once you've received Jesus into your heart, His Spirit lives inside of you, and you can learn to hear Him. "My sheep hear My voice, and I know them, and they follow Me." John 10:27; NKJV

1

NO OFFENSE

When Life Doesn't Make Sense

She was judged as the wrong race, the wrong socioeconomic status, the wrong religion, and the wrong gender. An outcast. Brushed aside and rejected by society. Devalued, discarded, and desperate beyond measure.

Have you ever felt like this? Have you ever looked at your circumstances, health issues, finances, or relationships and thought, *I have no ability to change this...what now?* The Canaanite woman from Matthew 15 likely had these thoughts over the years.

> "'Have mercy on me, O Lord, Son of David! My daughter is severely demon-possessed.'
> His disciples urged Him to send her away and Jesus answered her not a word... until He said,
> 'I was not sent except to the lost sheep of the house of Israel.'
> She worshipped Him saying, 'Lord, help me!'
> He answered and said,

'It is not good to take the children's bread and throw it to the little dogs.'
And she said,
'Yes, Lord, yet even the little dogs eat the crumbs which fall from their master's table.'
Then Jesus said to her,
'O woman, great is your faith! Let it be to you as you desire.' And her daughter was healed from that very hour."
Matthew 15:22-28; NKJV, paraphrased

This story, on the surface, often offends people. Let's look at it more closely and see Jesus' heart behind the words that He said. Jesus often says things we don't understand, or He is silent when He wants us to dig deeper and find a mystery that He has planted for us. Consider the Canaanite woman... what might she have felt? What did she tap into—in Jesus—that propelled her to keep pressing in?

THE CANAANITE WOMAN'S STORY

Perhaps these thoughts crossed her mind...[3]

Crying out for the deliverance of my daughter, I begged,
"Lord, we have been cruelly oppressed and afflicted
and have tried everything we know to do."

But He did not answer me a word.
"Did He hear me?" I wondered.
"Does He care?"
"Will He bring deliverance after all these years?"

Then those closest to Him, annoyed by my desperation,
implored Him to shun me—casting me off again.

---

[3] Using a creative nonfiction style of writing, I imagined what the Canaanite woman might have thought as she relentlessly pursued God for her miracle.

But for this I am grateful.
Perhaps it was *this*—the injustice of their shaming—
that spurred Him to speak.

Although the words He spoke seemed like a wall,
through the gaze of His eyes I saw a door.
He was inciting me, beckoning me.
So I went back to what I had observed about the Son of David:
He is merciful, and He is just.

Seeing His heart ignited my faith.
He is for me.

He had to know that this delayed healing for my daughter's deliverance had wrought great brokenness in our lives.
Oppression and chronic pain are a cruel injustice.
With locking eyes, I pleaded boldly,
"Lord, help me!"

Again I saw the paradox.
His words said, "No."
No? I could have gotten angry.
I could have been insulted, offended even.

But in His eyes there was no offense.
As He spoke the "no," I saw an invitation in His gaze.

Would I pull on His goodness, justice, and mercy?
Or would I let my broken history and experience dictate my response?

As His words hung in the air, He leaned in,
Ever so slightly, but I saw it.
There was something more,
like He was expecting—hoping for—a response from me.

I felt like I had nothing.
How does one respond when the Deliverer says, "No?"

But then, against all odds, I stepped in.
I stepped into the door of His eyes.
Somehow just looking at Him filled me with strength and hope
and brought a clarity that I'd never known.

Secrets are revealed in the secret place of His gaze.
Seeing Him see me gave me the courage to respond,
"Oh Lord, Your mercy is so great and Your goodness so abundant
that I ask—again—for my daughter's healing."

He smiled, nodded, and said to me,
"You have seen My heart and believed.
Your faith is great; it shall be done for you as you wish."

Then my daughter was healed, delivered, and set free that very hour.

At some point you will run into a situation where you need God to show up for you. There will be something for which you are asking Him that you have no capacity to make happen. What do you do when you don't get the answer you're praying for? Do you become hurt? Confused? Angry? Offended? The story of the Canaanite woman shows us how to avoid these pitfalls, see from God's perspective, and find our victory.

We each must learn to deal with our disappointments… or offense will seep in like poison. Offense is a tactic of the enemy to:

- blind you to the truth;
- disable you;
- and build walls in your heart that cut off your hope.

We cannot afford to live stuck in offense.[4] If you find yourself here, Jesus invites you to lean in and see His heart, like the Canaanite woman did.

UNDERSTANDING THE STAKES

Rich or poor, educated or uneducated, male or female, offense is no respecter of persons. The Canaanite woman was outcast by society—tempted with offense.

In Matthew 11 we see another, John the Baptist, esteemed by society—but also tempted with offense. Let's look at the backdrop of John's story.

His elderly parents, who had endured decades of disappointment and shame from being barren, were given the Word of the Lord that they would have a miracle son. This announcement, where the angel Gabriel prophesied John's birth, created great expectation for his life.

> "For he will be great in the sight of the LORD... He will also be filled with the Holy Spirit, even from his mother's womb. And he will turn many of the children of Israel to the LORD their God. He will also go before Him in the spirit and power of Elijah, 'to turn the hearts of the fathers to the children,' and the disobedient to the wisdom of the just, to make ready a people prepared for the LORD." Luke 1:15-17; NKJV

How many times did John's parents recount this to him? How often did they talk about the call of God on his life? Yes, he was raised knowing the greatness of his purpose. His life exuded the supernatural power of God as he prepared the way for Jesus the Messiah. And yet... when Herod threw him in prison, he had questions:

---

[4] Many of the concepts I share about the Canaanite woman and John the Baptist I gleaned from Pastor Bill Johnson—who taught on the importance of not being offended.

- Of course the Messiah would save him—wouldn't He?
- Jesus would surely exercise His power and deliver him—wouldn't He?

"And when John had heard in prison about the works of Christ, he sent two of his disciples and said to Him, 'Are You the Coming One, or do we look for another?'

Jesus answered and said to them, 'Go and tell John the things which you hear and see: The blind see and the lame walk; the lepers are cleansed and the deaf hear; the dead are raised up and the poor have the gospel preached to them. And blessed is he who is not offended because of Me.'" Matthew 11:2-6; NKJV

John was the son of a priest. He knew Old Testament prophecies, like Isaiah 35 and 61, that described what the Messiah would do. John understood by Jesus' answer in Matthew 11 that He was declaring Himself to be the Messiah.[5]

And yet, John was in prison. He was not experiencing the freedom that Christ was bringing to those around him. He, no doubt, prayed earnestly. Yet, there he sat behind bars. When John inquired of Jesus, he got what—on the surface—seems to be an odd response: "Blessed is the one who is not offended because of Me." Why would that be Jesus' answer to John?

Jesus gave him and gives us this exhortation because He knows the stakes are high for living in offense. Jesus knew that if John were to be offended, he would be opening the door to the plans of the enemy. Satan, the enemy of our souls, knows that offense is a stumbling block that hinders our connection with God and impedes our ability to hear Him clearly. Since satan's goal is to disconnect us from God, we need to be on guard, as he will surely tempt us with offense.

---

[5] John knew Jesus was the Messiah. He testified of Him in John 1:29-35.

He will mockingly accuse God to you, whispering lies such as:
- "If God cared, He would come through for you—wouldn't He?"
- "If God were good, He would deliver you—wouldn't He?"
- "If God had your best at heart, He would change your situation—wouldn't He?"
- "If God loved you, how could He let this happen to you?"

The enemy wants you to think that God isn't coming through for you, and he wants you to be hurt and resentful. However, if you see yourself—and your situation—from God's perspective, you will have everything you need to overcome.

GOD IS FOR YOU

God's purposes for you are always good. Even when you don't understand why things look the way they do in your life. We all want the deliverance that the Canaanite woman received. But, what happens when our story looks more like John the Baptist's? John sought for Jesus to deliver him, but Herod killed him. He did not get breakthrough during his natural life. What do we do with that? Can we rely on God? We will see that God is for us and that the answers to these tough questions are only found *in His presence.*

Hebrews 6 tells us that there are two unchangeable things that we can depend on, especially in the difficult times.
1) We can rely on the **nature of God**—His character and essence. He is unchanging, just, merciful, and completely faithful.
2) We can rely on **His oath**—His Word, His promise, His truth. He cannot lie, so when God says something we can believe it.

"Because God wanted to make the unchanging **nature** of His purpose very clear to the heirs of what was promised, He confirmed it with an **oath**. God did this so that, by two unchangeable things in which it is impossible for God to lie, we [who]... take hold of the

hope set before us may be greatly encouraged."
Hebrews 6:17-18; NIV, bold added

In Scripture we see how the **nature of His character** and the **oath of His Word** are anchors that will secure your soul. To the degree that you know Him and believe what He says will be the degree to which you are encouraged in the ups and downs of life.

"...[M]y soul is downcast within me.
Yet this I call to mind
and therefore I have hope:
Because of the LORD's great love we are not consumed,
for His compassions never fail.
They are new every morning;
 great is Your faithfulness." Lamentations 3:20b-23; NIV

"Fear not, for I have redeemed you;
I have called you by your name;
You are Mine.
When you pass through the waters, I will be with you;
And through the rivers, they shall not overflow you.
When you walk through the fire, you shall not be burned,
Nor shall the flame scorch you.
For I am the LORD your God,
The Holy One of Israel, your Savior..." Isaiah 43:1b-3a; NKJV

"The LORD is merciful and gracious,
Slow to anger, and abounding in mercy." Psalm 103:8; NKJV

I love God's faithfulness, redemption, and mercy, but there are two other attributes that have helped me trust Him in my most challenging times: His justice and righteousness. *He will always do what is right.* Even when things don't make sense, His very nature is to bring justice and righteousness to our lives. His rule is built upon it. You can rely on it.

"Righteousness and justice are the foundation of Your throne; steadfast love and faithfulness go before You." Psalm 89:14; ESV

"'I will betroth you to Me forever;
Yes, I will betroth you to Me
In righteousness and justice,
In lovingkindness and mercy;
I will betroth you to Me in faithfulness,
And you shall know the LORD.
'It shall come to pass in that day
That I will answer,' says the LORD..." Hosea 2:19-21a; NKJV

These rich verses declare who God is on our behalf. They describe how it is possible to step into victory even in our darkest, most desperate times. You will have afflictions in life. You will experience disappointments. People will hurt you and treat you wrongly. But God will lead you into victory in Christ.

"Now thanks be to God who always leads us in triumph in Christ, and through us diffuses the fragrance of His knowledge in every place." 2 Corinthians 2:14; NKJV

This is a great promise, but how does it play out in the valleys of your life?

• How do you connect to Him when you're struggling with hurt and disillusionment?

• How can you live in victory when you're not experiencing God's deliverance, healing, or freedom in some area of your life?

• What do you stand on when you're in pain—when you can barely stand?

KEY TO VICTORY

➤ Connect to the Nature of God

The Canaanite woman found her breakthrough by connecting to the person of God. She stepped into His nature and relied on His character. She pushed everything else out of her sight—the seeming rejection of Jesus, the annoyance of the disciples, her own fears and disappointment.

She silenced all of that and focused on the One in front of her. She locked onto His gaze. She fixed herself on Him—on His justice and mercy. And in that sacred moment, she experienced something that allowed her to more deeply believe for the impossible.

And although being with Him may not immediately change your circumstances, it will change how you see them. It will change you. It's in this place that He will fill you with Himself; it is here that you have access to everything He is and everything He has. This is where your victory begins. This is where you crush the head of the enemy—in the midst of your loss, right in the middle of what isn't working.

> "'Then you will call upon Me and go and pray to Me, and I will listen to you. And you will seek Me and find Me, when you search for Me with all your heart. I will be found by you,' says the LORD..." Jeremiah 29:12-14a; NKJV

> "Draw near to God and He will draw near to you..." James 4:8a; NKJV

> "Because he has set his love upon Me, therefore I will deliver him;
> I will set him on high, because he has known My name.
> He shall call upon Me, and I will answer him;
> I will be with him in trouble;

I will deliver him and honor him.
With long life I will satisfy him,
And show him My salvation." Psalm 91:14-16; NKJV

"When You said, 'Seek My face,'
My heart said to You, 'Your face, LORD, I will seek.'
...I would have lost heart, unless I had believed
That I would see the goodness of the LORD
In the land of the living." Psalm 27:8, 13; NKJV

MESSAGE FROM GOD'S HEART:

"My child, why would you think that I am not on your side to bring good to you? Why would you think that I wouldn't move heaven and earth for you?

    I would.
    I do.
    In fact, I already have.
    I already moved heaven and earth for you.
    I already gave everything.

There is literally nothing more that I could do for you or give to you that I haven't already done or given.

Believe this.

Believe this with all your heart because it's the truest truth.
What I did for you is who I am on your behalf.

    It's My heart for you.
    It's My promise over you.
    It's My commitment to you… and it will not change.

You can trust that I will not—I cannot—go against Myself, ever.

Therefore, you can count on it.
You can count on Me.
You can know that I only have your best at hand.

And when you don't see Me coming through for you, consider what you're looking at.
Shift your gaze.
Move from looking at your circumstances to looking at Me.
Look to Me.

When you lock into My presence and seek My face, you will:
 See My character;
 Receive My mercy;
 Find My justice;
 Embrace My promise;
 And be assured of My goodness again."

2

DREAM BIG

Deferred Dreams Aligned

Consider the hopes and dreams you have. What is in your heart to do in life? What do you value? God has put dreams deep within each of us that identify what He created us to do. But what happens when your big dream eludes you?

- What do you do when you've done everything you can and it's still out of reach?
- What do you do after years of waiting?
- How do you continue to contend for this thing without getting caught in disappointment?

EMMI'S STORY

Ever since Emmi was a little girl, she wanted to get married and have a family of her own. There was something deep within her that longed for this dream. It may not have seemed like a big deal to many, but the desire was strong in her. It was more than just wanting family. She felt like her destiny hinged upon it.

She knew she could not settle. She knew that whomever she married would have to be aligned with God and His purposes. So she pursued Him as she looked for the right man. She intentionally looked... at high school... college... church... work... ministry and social events... and yet, she met no potential husband.

She went to dozens of bridal showers and weddings as she celebrated her friends finding their mates, and she longed, looked, and waited for the fulfillment of her dream. As the years turned into decades, her heart ached, and she cried out to the Lord.

And because she'd wanted to get married from such a young age, turning thirty was a particularly difficult marker. Then, when she turned thirty-five, still with no prospects, she began to ask the hard questions. "Father, where is the one You gave me vision for—who I've been praying for all these years? God, did I miss it? What's the hold-up? I feel like life is passing me by..."

She believed that God promised her marriage and children. She believed He was faithful to fulfill His Word. So what was the purpose of all this waiting? Why were so many around her living her dream? This is where her questions prompted her to dig deeper.

"Lord, what are You doing in my life? I'm so tired of waiting. Show me Your plan." As she cried out, God began to speak to her heart.

> "Come, sit with Me, and write down what you hear My Spirit saying to you. I will speak to you."

* Once you've accepted Jesus into your heart, He will lead and guide you through His written and spoken Word. Every believer has the capacity to hear from God. Sometimes it's just a sense about what you should or shouldn't do. Sometimes it's actually words. The more time you spend with Him, the more clearly you will hear His voice.

"My sheep hear My voice, and I know them, and they follow Me." John 10:27; NKJV

"But he answered, 'It is written, "Man shall... live by... every word that comes from the mouth of God.""" Matthew 4:4; ESV

"It is the Spirit who gives life; the flesh is no help at all. The words that I have spoken to you are spirit and life." John 6:63; ESV

So Emmi got a journal and began writing what she felt like the Holy Spirit was saying to her. Initially it felt awkward to risk writing what she felt like she heard. She questioned it. Was she really hearing from God? Or was she making it up? As she sat in His presence and considered what she sensed Him saying she began to embrace it. It was in alignment with Scripture, and what she heard infused her with hope.[6]

These are some of the things He began to say to her,
> "My daughter, the first thing I want to do in your life is establish your identity. I want you to know who you are. I want you to know how I see you. I want you to live from that place of blessing and security.

> Let Me fill you. Look to Me. I know you want to get married and have a family. And you will. But do not look to that as your fulfillment. Look to Me. I am your Strong Tower, your covering, your hope and your joy. I am your fulfillment."

One of the themes He spoke to her often was the message of love. He'd say,
> "*I* love you. I *love* you. I love *you*, My daughter. Take it in. You're My girl. You are Mine. I purposefully created you for good. You delight Me. You are My beloved. I have all that concerns you. You

---

[6] This felt like confirmation that what she was hearing was from God, because at that time in her life her own thoughts/self-talk were not that hopeful or encouraging.

have not missed what I have intended for you. I am doing a deeper thing in you. This 'wait time' is intentional."

God began to show Emmi things from *His* perspective. The more time she spent with Him, the more she understood that this life was much bigger than simply achieving her dream. He showed her how her victory hinged on what she focused upon. Focusing on the Almighty One settled her heart. It was only when she looked around at what she didn't have that she felt lack and sadness.

When Emmi did finally meet the man that God confirmed was to be her husband, she was so excited to see her dreams finally coming to fruition. She got married at thirty-seven years old, full of expectation.

MORE WAITING?

But she was surprised to find herself in another season of delay as she had a difficult time getting pregnant—which confounded her as she thought she'd already "put her time in" waiting for her spouse. She was sure that God's abundant blessing would come and she'd finally get to enjoy her heart's desire. Why more delay? God put this desire for family deep within her heart. Plus, she had received numerous prophetic words[7] about having children.

When she was thirty-nine, she finally got pregnant. She was elated. Thrilled! Grateful beyond words. She had so much vision for this life within her. She prayed for and prophesied over this baby. She felt like it was a little girl, and she loved her. But then... she started to miscarry. How could that happen with God's blessing and all the promises He'd given to her? She prayed with all her might, with all her faith. She rallied the troops—her pastors, family and friends—believing that God

---

[7] God gives prophetic words to people for the purpose of exhortation, edification, and comfort—often regarding a promise He has for them.

would turn this around. But He didn't. She lost the life within her. And it was devastating.

She was surprised at how tangible her grief was. She had a difficult time breathing. Sadness and loss gripped the deepest places of her being, and she wrestled with anger and hopelessness. She asked God, "Why was this loss allowed to happen? We dedicated this life to You!" She felt empty.

She wondered, *If God didn't sustain my pregnancy—which is my biggest dream—can I trust Him with anything? If He didn't intervene here, will He come through in other areas of my life?* Emmi was grateful for the foundation of all those years she'd waited upon God and heard His heart for her, but this loss shook her to the core. It showed her that she still had some holes within her where she really didn't know or trust God.

Every month was a roller coaster. Every month was a hope-filled, hope-dashed time. It took another year and a half before Emmi got pregnant again. And, although she felt incredible joy, she had to push thoughts of fear away. She knew she did not want the enemy to have any ground in her life and she could not afford to let in any of his thoughts. She pressed into God, in hope against hope, and chose to believe. She chose faith.

She went to her first doctor's appointment and got blood work done, which showed good levels for a healthy pregnancy. Everything was on track! She was so grateful. She loved being pregnant. Then, she went in for her first ultrasound. There was no heartbeat. *No!!! Not again!* She refused to believe this could happen again.

She began to speak life over her womb. She knew Romans 8:11. The same Spirit that raised Jesus from the dead lived inside of her, and she would tap into His resurrection power and believe Him to bring life back into her womb. She believed with all of her heart, and she did not miscarry. Weeks turned into months, and she continued to believe. But when she went back to her doctor, who did two more ultrasounds, there was still no heartbeat. For some reason just the placenta continued to grow. The doctor highly recommended having a D & C (dilation and curettage).

After lots of prayer and with the urging of her husband, she agreed. There are no words to describe how difficult this was to do. The loss threatened to consume her. There were no answers. Asking "why?" got her nowhere.

As compassionate as people were, no one seemed to understand how strong this dream of hers was, this dream that was always just out of reach. What do you do when you cannot attain your biggest heart's desire? What do you do with your heart? How could Emmi live and not become hopeless? Now in her forties, the chance of her getting pregnant was decreasing.

She went before God again. "Lord, I believe You have me—and everything that concerns me—but what are You doing here? This did not take you by surprise, but I don't understand. I feel so ripped off, so robbed by the enemy."

As painful as it was, she knew she needed to lean into God and hear what He was saying to her. Could she hear Him through her pain? She didn't know, but she set aside time to sit with Him. She got her journal, tucked away with Him—in her brokenness—and asked Him to speak to her.

She spent much time seeking Him as she needed to know His heart. She needed His presence to fill her. Day after day, she pursued Him. And as she did, He poured into her. Somehow, His love soaked into those shattered places, and she was able to receive His comfort. But what about His truth? What was the answer as to why this second huge loss had occurred? This is when God brought her to a verse in

Isaiah 40 that has become a marker for her life when things don't make sense.

> "Why do you say, O Jacob,
> And speak, O Israel:
> 'My way is hidden from the LORD,
> And my just claim is passed over by my God'?
> Have you not known?
> Have you not heard?
> The everlasting God, the LORD,
> The Creator of the ends of the earth,
> neither faints nor is weary.
> His understanding is unsearchable." Isaiah 40:27-28; NKJV

God spoke to her heart,
> "Oh, My precious Em,
> why do you think that your way is hidden from Me?
> Why do you think that I have passed over your 'just claim'?
> Yes, it is a just claim to have children, but... do you not know?
> Have you not heard?
> I am everlasting.
> I made everything—from nothing.
> Do you think I can't do that again?
> Do you think that anything is too difficult for Me?
> Nothing is too big, difficult, or too much for Me.
> And My understanding is so far beyond yours.

If something does not make sense to you, it's because you simply do not see the whole picture yet.

When you don't understand, it just means that what is happening is bigger than your current frame of reference.

Do you think that Abraham and Sarah understood why they had to wait so long for their promised son?

They did not understand.
But know that I had purpose in My timing for them.
And I have purpose in My timing in your life too.

I always have purpose—especially when I am doing a big thing.

If you wait upon Me and keep your heart before Me, not only can I accomplish My plan in you, but I will use this priceless time to develop something within you that can be forged in no other way."

This truth became a foundation that Emmi began to rebuild her life upon. She began to believe that:
- God was doing something that she could not yet see.
- God understood things that she did not yet understand.

Spending time in His presence allowed her to know that He was worthy of her trust—even in the loss. Maybe this, maybe choosing to trust Him, was more foundational to her destiny than her actual dream.

HEARTBREAK OR OPPORTUNITY?

One day, feeling a wave of desire for children again she said, "Lord, not having children has been the biggest heartbreak of my life." It was not a bitter statement. It was simply a heart-wrenching acknowledgment of an unfulfilled dream that had turned into an impossibility. As she lingered in that moment, she tangibly felt the holy weightiness of God. In her spirit she could see His compassionate eyes intently looking at her, and He nodded. After the most tender pause, she sensed Him gently saying,

"Yes, my beloved one, it could be your biggest heartbreak... or it could be your biggest opportunity. Instead of letting this disappointment define you, you could see it from My vantage point. You could choose to love Me above your greatest desire.

For My precious one, you have no idea how valuable the gift of your heart is to Me. Loving Me in this place is your most powerful testimony. Right now you cannot see the weight of that, but it is the most priceless gift that you have to give Me; and it will be a part of your legacy for all of eternity.

So every time you think of your loss, of what you don't yet have, put it on the altar and choose to love Me in its place. This sacrifice is truly the sweetest incense to Me. And I will not leave you lacking. Oh, My beloved one, if you let Me, I will surely fill you. I will pour My love into every part of you. And you will know the greatest of joy in it. This is the mystery and beauty of the sacrifice."

God gave Emmi a life-giving perspective shift in that interaction. She found that the more time she spent with Him, the easier it was to hear Him. This strengthened and encouraged her greatly. This is the nature of hearing God's heart. Just like it brought life to her so it will bring life and hope to you too.

Hearing from the Lord will both enable you to believe for the impossible and allow you to give your heart's desires back to God. Even now in her fifties, the dream of having children has not diminished, so she continues to believe for them. What will that look like? Emmi has no idea—for it's no longer the focus of her life. Children could come as a supernatural miracle like they did for Sarah, Elizabeth, and Hannah; or through adoption; or in some other unlikely way...

She has learned to live on the altar, offering her love to God as a continual sacrifice. The choice that He gave her—to view her deferred dream as either a heartbreak or an opportunity—is a choice that you too will have to make at some point in your life. Your big dream is the very thing that God may use to test and refine you—to give you a chance to love and trust Him with your whole heart.

Choosing God above your dream does not mean that it will not happen. He gave it to you to fulfill it. The process may not be easy, but choosing to love God more than your big dream will usher you into your greatest victory.

If God has put something in your heart, believe for it. It may look different than you thought it would; the timing might be different than you wanted it to be. But if you keep God's heart before you, you will be surprised how He sustains you in the waiting.

> "The LORD is my strength and my shield;
> my heart trusts in Him, and He helps me.
> My heart leaps for joy,
> and with my song I praise Him." Psalm 28:7; NIV

> "...God is the strength of my heart and my portion forever." Psalm 73:26b; ESV

KEY TO VICTORY

➢ Hear God's heart for you

Hearing God's heart for you is your lifeline, your plumb line. He will give you wisdom and clarity. He wants to share His Kingdom perspective with you.

Listening to the still, small voice of God will strengthen, empower, and sustain you.

Even the mighty prophet Elijah was discouraged after Jezebel threatened his life. 1 Kings 19 describes how it was the voice of the Lord that realigned him.

> "The LORD said, 'Go out and stand on the mountain in the presence of the LORD...' Then a great and powerful wind tore the mountains apart and shattered the rocks before the LORD, but

the LORD was not in the wind. After the wind there was an earthquake, but the LORD was not in the earthquake. After the earthquake came a fire, but the LORD was not in the fire. And after the fire came a gentle whisper. When Elijah heard it, he... stood at the mouth of the cave." 1 Kings 19:11-13a; NIV

God gave Elijah encouragement and direction through the quiet intimacy of His voice. God is personal, and most often the answers He has for us come through a personal relationship—through both His written and spoken Word.

"The voice of the LORD is powerful; the voice of the LORD is majestic." Psalm 29:4; NIV

"I will stand my watch...
And watch to see what He will say to me...
Then the LORD answered me and said:
'Write the vision
And make it plain on tablets,
That he may run who reads it.'" Habakkuk 2:1-2; NKJV

This verse encourages us to not only hear but to write down what God shows us as we seek Him. When He whispers a word in your spirit, write it down. As I began to personally do this, my relationship with God grew tremendously. Writing what I feel like He is saying to me allows me to record, and test, what I hear.

What does this look like?
- Journal what you feel like He is saying to you.

- Then, re-read it and make sure that it is in alignment with His written Word. This is your greatest safeguard.

If anything you hear goes against what He has said in Scripture, discard it. God will never contradict His Word.

MESSAGE FROM GOD'S HEART:

"It's true, My mighty one. I put something deep within your heart to accomplish on the earth, as you partner with Me.

Your big dream is unique to you—to your gifts and talents, to your abilities and preferences.
It's something I specifically put within you.
So, do not give up on it.
Do not shy away from it.
Do not get weary from it not coming to fruition more easily.
There is a process in it for you that's as important as the dream itself.

Above all, I want you to know Me in it.
I want you to be filled with My goodness for you.
I want you to live in My freedom and truth.
Be careful not to compare your life with anyone else's.
I have a special place and a special path for you to walk with Me.

It is beautiful.
It is ours.
And it will be your testimony for all of eternity.
So, as you embrace Me, embrace this journey we are on together.

Learn to hear Me.
I will speak to you.
I will encourage you.
I will show you the way to walk."

3

MORE THAN ENOUGH

Finding God's Provision

Is there an area of your life where you feel lack, where you feel like you don't have what you need? What do you do when you don't have enough? What do you do when:

- your finances aren't covering your bills?
- you're lacking relational connections?
- you don't have the education you need to advance at work?

The enemy will come against you, mocking God in your mind and whispering how God does not care about you or what you need. The enemy wants you to doubt God's provision in your life. Why? Because he knows that God's provision allows you to feel valued, cared for, and loved. And the enemy wants you to doubt that; he wants you to feel neglected and forsaken.

JESSE'S STORY

From as early as he could remember, Jesse felt like something had been stolen from him. Something was taken that he could never get back. He learned at a young age that life is not fair and what happens is often out of our control.

When he was four years old, while simply going to the grocery store with his mom, a car sideswiped them and in an instant the trajectory of his life was changed forever. Through the impact of that violent crash, Jesse lost the normalcy of his childhood. He lost that carefree time of just going to the park, racing Hot Wheels, and going to friends' birthday parties. Instead he was stuck in the hospital, experiencing a level of pain he could not understand.

As a result of that crash Jesse lost about four inches of his left leg. It was crushed beyond repair. The doctors gave his parents two choices:
- Jesse could have a surgery where they'd put a metal rod in his leg. This however, would require that as he grew he would have to have multiple surgeries. The doctors advised against this because of the substantial and long-term risks that were likely to occur.
- The parents' other option was to have the shattered section of Jesse's leg removed and fit him with an orthotic shoe lift that he'd have to wear for the rest of his life. This is what his parents chose for him.

The surgery and recovery time were painful, lonely, and scary. And even though his parents did what they could to encourage him, by the time he had physically recovered he was aware of how different he was from other kids. He wanted friends but didn't know how to connect. Being in the hospital during that critical time where kids learn how to read social cues and play together left a hole in his development. Of course he didn't know that at the time; he just always felt different. He so wished he could fit in.

And then there was the reality that people often didn't know what to do with "different." Jesse could not hide his disability. Having a four-inch lift gave him a substantial limp and made running, and even play-ing, difficult. As hard as he tried to be normal, he often tripped and fell. Kids at school laughed at him; many ignored him. Everywhere he went he noticed that people stared at him. This made him extremely self-conscious, and by the time he was in middle school he had be-come socially awkward and isolated.

By the time he graduated from high school, he felt substantially stuck. What was he supposed to do in life? How was he going to make a living for himself? He didn't know, so he settled into a menial job—that he didn't like—just to get by. Emotional and relational lack had characterized his life. Now he was barely able to make ends meet. He noted the correlation between his inability to financially flourish and feeling devalued. Jesse was surprised to see how lack had eroded his confidence. It thwarted him from stepping out and taking risks in life.

Could Things Ever Change?

One day while watching TV, Jesse saw a program about a master artist that fascinated him. The way the artist mixed and used colors to cre-ate something out of nothing ignited something in him. The artist's expression was powerful and free, and it drew Jesse in. He felt a wisp of hope. Maybe he could do art. Maybe he could be powerful and free too.

He got some supplies and began to create. He drew and painted what-ever came from within him. He tapped into the deepest parts of his heart and expressed them. Most of his initial art was full of pain. But the more he created, the stronger he felt. It was through expressing himself artistically that he felt like he finally had a point of connection within himself. Jesse studied different art forms and styles and became very good very quickly. He flourished as he created.

Because art was such a life-giving place for him, he spent the majority of his time doing it. This was good for his soul; however, he still had the issue of interacting with others and still struggled with his finances. As much as he loved art he doubted he could make a living with it.

One day while flipping through YouTube looking for videos on design, Jesse stumbled upon what he thought was a motivational speaker. He reflected, *I could use some inspiration today*. So he decided to listen to the program.

Interestingly, in the midst of the speaker giving some practical advice, he began to talk about God. What he said intrigued Jesse. Jesse didn't grow up in a home that believed in God. As he listened, though, he was drawn to what the speaker was saying. He talked about how God created each person for a purpose—for good. The more he spoke, the more Jesse leaned in. *Could this be true? Is there good for me?* he wondered. *Could the broken places in my life be restored? Could God be real?*

He decided to look online hoping to find out more about God. He watched many other videos where people talked about who God was and how much He loved everyone. They told stories about how He had intervened in their lives. As Jesse listened, an excitement rose up within him. This is what his heart had longed for his whole life—to be genuinely loved. *I don't know if God is true, he thought, but my life isn't working well now. What do I have to lose?*

So Jesse, with a hesitant excitement, stepped out and typed in his search bar, "Who is God?" and "Who does God say I am?" These verses popped up.

> "Just as He chose us in Him before the foundation of the world... having predestined us to adoption as sons by Jesus Christ to Himself, according to the good pleasure of His will... He made us accepted in the Beloved." Ephesians 1:4a, 5, 6b; NKJV

> "But you are... His own special people, that you may proclaim the

praises of Him who called you out of darkness into His marvelous light; who once were not a people but are now the people of God, who had not obtained mercy but now have obtained mercy."
1 Peter 2:9; NKJV

"Therefore, if anyone is in Christ, he is a new creation; old things have passed away; behold, all things have become new."
2 Corinthians 5:17; NKJV

These verses were life to Jesse's dry, malnourished soul. The more time he spent researching what God said, the more he wanted to know about this God. Something was stirring inside of him, propelling him to dig deeper. He decided to get a Bible. As he read he was captivated. Something was becoming alive within him.

He almost couldn't identify what had changed until he saw a documentary about lions. He had always felt alone and rejected. Meeting God began to shift his mindset. Jesse felt like he had been invited into the protective social structure of the lion's pride; he finally felt like he belonged.

He was thrilled to notice how his perspective changed once he connected with God. The hurtful looks didn't necessarily stop, but when someone reacted to his disfigured leg, Jesse didn't internalize it like he used to. Instead he encouraged himself by reciting phrases from different verses that he'd read.

- If God is for me, who can be against me? Romans 8:31
- It is God who justifies. Who is he who condemns?
Romans 8:33-34
- Who shall separate me from the love of Christ? Romans 8:35
- Lord, You created me for good. 1 Timothy 4:4; Ephesians 2:10
- You lead and guide me. Psalm 31:3
- You restore my soul. Psalm 23:2
- You show me Your truth. Psalm 25:4-5

- I am your child. John 1:12
- I have the mind of Christ. Philippians 2:5
- In You I have wisdom. Colossians 2:2-3

Once Jesse anchored into God's Word and began declaring its truth over his life, he became more and more secure in his identity. This allowed him to interact with others more confidently. He started to believe that he was valuable and that his art had value. He began to believe that he had a purpose—something important to contribute.

As Jesse stepped into who God said he was, he could finally risk putting his art out for others to see. This was scary, but it opened up some relational connections that brought healing to his soul. And when he started to feel intimidated to meet new people, he remembered God's promises. The more he believed what God said, the more he trusted God's provision in every area of his life, including his finances. As this trust grew, Jesse stepped out—both relationally in connecting with others, and in finding places to share his art.

This wasn't a quick or easy process; but as he committed to it, he began to believe that he would experience God's provision. As he did, he noticed that people genuinely enjoyed spending time with him—which opened the door for him to sell more of his art. His life went from one of extensive lack to one of fulfillment and connection.

FINANCIAL PROVISION

God promises to care for you; He promises to meet your needs. He is your provision. In fact, one of the names God revealed to Abraham describes Him as: "The-LORD-Will-Provide." This also is His commitment to you.

> "So Abraham called that place 'The LORD Will Provide.' And to this day it is said, 'On the mountain of the LORD it will be pro-

vided.'" Genesis 22:14; NIV

The truth we can all depend on is that "on the mountain of the LORD, **it will be provided**." Whatever your "it" is, God is your provision. When you live "on His mountain"—which means living in His presence—His promise is that He will give you what you need.

"And my God shall supply all your needs according to His riches in glory by Christ Jesus." Philippians 4:19; NKJV

"As His divine power has given to us all things that pertain to life and godliness, through the knowledge of Him who called us by glory and virtue, by which have been given to us exceedingly great and precious promises..." 2 Peter 1:3-4a; NKJV

"If you, imperfect as you are, know how to lovingly take care of your children and give them what's best, how much more ready is your heavenly Father to give wonderful gifts to those who ask him?" Matthew 7:11; TPT

Whether you are experiencing lack in your relationships, finances, or any other area, God's living, active, all-powerful Word contains your answer. When you apply His truth to your life you can expect things to shift.

Key to Victory

➤ Declare God's Word

Declaring God's Word will:
- bring truth and alignment to you;
- open doors for you;
- renew your perspective.

"For the Word of God is living and powerful..."
Hebrews 4:12a; NKJV

"Every Scripture has been written by the Holy Spirit, the breath of God. It will empower you by its instruction and correction, giving you the strength to take the right direction..."
2 Timothy 3:16; TPT

"Your word is a lamp to my feet
And a light to my path." Psalm 119:105; NKJV

"...So shall My Word be that goes forth from My mouth;
It shall not return to Me void,
But it shall accomplish what I please,
And it shall prosper in the thing for which I sent it."
Isaiah 55:11; NKJV

Because we connect to God through His Word, the enemy will do whatever he can to keep you from reading it. He will tell you that it's boring and a waste of time. If you have a difficult time reading Scripture,[8] ask God to reveal Himself to you in it. He will.

• He will activate His living Word within you.

• His Word will empower you to overcome the attacks of the enemy in your life.

"Therefore put on the full armor of God, so that when the day of evil comes, you may be able to stand your ground... take up the shield of faith, with which you can extinguish all the flaming arrows of the evil one. Take the helmet of salvation and the sword of the Spirit, which is the Word of God."
Ephesians 6:13a, 16b-17; NIV

---

[8] One thing I've found that has ignited my desire to read Scripture is Psalm 119. I have repeatedly seen this Psalm draw people to God's Word.

MESSAGE FROM GOD'S HEART:

"Oh, My beloved one, I know all that you've been through.
I know the areas where you have:
- been treated wrongfully;
- been hurt;
- experienced lack.

I am here to show you how to step out of these traumas and into My abundance.

I have already given you what you need to flourish.
Believe this.
Receive it.
Build yourself up in My Word so that when the enemy comes against you,you are prepared to overcome his attacks.

Let Me tell you who you are.
Let Me fill you.
Let Me show you how to step up, so you can risk sharing the gifts I've put within you.
Your gifts, talents, and abilities are needed.
I gave them to you to share with the world; sharing what I've put within you will make the world a better place.

Don't play it safe.
Trust that I have you.
Trust I will provide everything you need.
In Me, you have more than enough.

Believe who I say you are, and go in My love and power."

4

CRIES OF THE HEART

Freedom from Emotional Issues

Whether emotionally or physically, at some point in your life, you will need healing. When you are in pain you likely pray for relief. But if you pray and the pain does not subside, what do you do?

Do you assume it's not God's will to heal you? Do you believe that you don't have enough faith? Do you think that God doesn't care? Or do you seek Him more intently as you contend for understanding and breakthrough?

MIA'S STORY

Mia was a kind, spunky youth who loved skateboarding, climbing trees, and hanging out with friends. Although for the most part she was a typical teenager, from a young age the truth was very important to her. She was fiercely intentional in all that she said and did.

Overall, life was good. Until it wasn't. One day, almost like a light switch had been flipped, Mia knew something was wrong. She had become incessantly thirsty, and no matter how much water she drank, she couldn't seem to quench her thirst. As a ninth-grade basketball player who was active in school, she hoped that it was just a fluke—but she knew something was off-kilter with her body. A gnawing fear lurked in her mind as she had a cousin who had Type 1 diabetes. *No, Lord. Please, not that...* she silently pleaded in her heart.

As days turned into weeks, she noticed that she was drinking excessive amounts of water and needed to use the bathroom an unreasonable number of times a day. She knew. She also knew that if she told her parents, she'd have to go to the doctor. Then the insulin shots would follow. She could not imagine having to do this every day. Feeling scared and overwhelmed, she prayed with all her heart.

Did God have an answer for her? She'd read Bible verses about healing, but until now she hadn't had a great need for it. That had all changed. Now she desperately sought for His tangible truth. If Jesus paid the price for her healing, like Scripture says, and if He healed *everyone* who asked Him when He lived on the earth,[9] surely He would heal her, wouldn't He? She believed He would. So she stepped out in young faith and asked Him to do for her what He did in those pages of the Bible.

Her faith began to waver, however, as each day gave her more evidence of the opposite. Then the day came when she was required to have a physical for the school sport she'd signed up for. She dreaded going to the appointment and tried to pretend she was fine.

But when her blood work came back, the doctor told her parents what she'd known all summer. Their plan was that she'd be admitted into the hospital for a few days to learn how to manage the diabetes and

---

[9] Psalm 103:1-5; Isaiah 53:4-5; 1 Peter 2:24; Acts 10:38

take insulin injections. This is where her desperate hoping turned upside down. This diagnosis triggered something deep within her that threatened her identity and value.

Mocking thoughts assailed her as she pictured people making fun of her for having to give herself shots. These thoughts morphed into irrational fear. Fear of rejection. *Who would want to be my friend?* Fear of pain. *How can I poke a metal needle into myself several times a day?* Fear of abandonment. *Why didn't God heal me? Doesn't He love me? Did I do something wrong?*

Although she didn't know it at the time, in her desperation, she began to listen to thoughts that were actually coming from the enemy of her soul. He taunted, *You shouldn't be a diabetic. You shouldn't have to take insulin. That's not fair. God's Word promises to heal you—doesn't it? You should be able to rely on that—shouldn't you? Maybe you didn't get healed yet because you didn't believe enough. Maybe you just need to try harder...* These thoughts echoed in her mind as they accused her. She didn't know, at fourteen, that if she heeded those thoughts they would infiltrate her mindset.

Mia tried to have more faith, but the more she stood on the "by His stripes I am healed" verses, such as Isaiah 53:5 and 1 Peter 2:24, the more fear she felt when she did not see her body responding. *What if I don't get healed?* She did not understand that true faith is accompanied by strength, hope, and joy—not the fear of, "What if it doesn't happen?" True faith isn't about what you can do; it's about stepping into what Jesus already did.

But since Mia didn't have a context for that yet, she bought into the thoughts the enemy was feeding her. And interestingly, the more she entertained these faulty thoughts, the more personified they became within her. One day, she realized she'd befriended them, embracing the destructive "help" they offered.

To Whom Are You Listening?

The enemy will personify his fiendish entourage of fear, anger, rebellion, etc. as traits that will empower you. He'll offer you their "strength" so that you embrace them before you see the deadly hook that's hidden within them. That's what happened to Mia.

Fear initially came as a friend who helped her build walls in her heart—offering to shield her from the pain she was so desperately trying to avoid. As Mia embraced the "protection" fear offered, she gave him an open door into her life. Fear then introduced her to anger. Anger justified and empowered her to dig her heels in and rebuff anyone who told her something she didn't want to hear. As she internalized anger she was able to push her parents and doctors away who pleaded with her to start taking insulin. Anger felt strong.

But the more "power" Mia got from him, the more he pushed and bullied *her*. He wanted her to be loud and obnoxious—which was not how she preferred to be. Anger, feeling like he was starting to lose his impact, decided to introduce Mia to one of his closest friends, rebellion. Rebellion taught her how to resist without being loud. He taught her how to give people cold, silent stares, which allowed her to feel like she was in control.

Sadly, the more she listened to these new "friends" of hers, the more distant everyone else around her became—including her family and friends at school and church. She noticed that ever since she'd embraced fear, anger, and rebellion, her world had become very small. Her life felt like it was disintegrating from the inside out. When she recognized this, she felt like the Holy Spirit prompted her to relinquish this entourage that came from the enemy. In her spirit she felt like God was calling her to let go of the contempt they stirred up within her.

God invited Mia into His truth and mercy. He held her heart that had been so lonely and broken in this whole process. So she asked Him, "What should I do? Your Word says that I am healed. I want to believe that. Diabetes is not in heaven, and Your Word says that we're to pray for things to be on earth as they are in heaven."[10]

Mia felt God's tenderness towards her in the midst of her brokenness, but because her foundation was skewed—and she'd already befriended the enemy's destructive companions—she could not hear God's voice clearly. Faulty thoughts justified her stance that refusing to go to the doctor and take medicine was faith. So she continued to strive for healing.

She demanded that her body align to the healing Scriptures she'd found, but she didn't understand that she was missing God's heart. She wanted the healing His Word promised, but the pain and disappointment she held onto blocked her from receiving His love.

She was not connecting well with God, and these new "friends" of hers were truly not good companions. They didn't ever wait to be invited in. Often fear and anger would crash in and assault her with irrational thoughts. They constantly tried to hijack her thinking and control what she said and did. Mia felt trapped in her body that wasn't working; and now she had a war going on in her mind.

It was here that she officially met one of fear's closest friends: shame. Shame had been lurking around from the very beginning, but Mia didn't recognize him until she already felt strong-armed by fear and his cohorts. As shame overshadowed her, she became inundated with rejection. It was shame that told her, *You'll never be normal. People will feel sorry for you. No one will want to marry you. At the core of who you are, you are broken. Flawed. You can't even live without medicine.*

---

[10] Jesus taught His disciples to pray: "Father... Your kingdom come, Your will be done, on earth as it is in heaven." Matthew 6:9a, 10; NIV

That was shame's voice. It was shame that told her she was deficient and she should hide this illness. Shame showed Mia how to live in the dark. Shame told her that she was bad—and unless she got rid of this disease that made her bad—she was worth less than others. Worthless.

When shame saw that Mia believed him, he knew it was time to introduce her to the ultimate kingpin in this whole process. Hiding his identity, this one coolly whispered, *If you can't get rid of this disease, your life will be miserable and you will never be happy so... why go through all the pain and rejection? What's the value of living? Wouldn't it be better to... just die?*

For the first time the thought seriously crossed Mia's mind. She didn't want to die. But she didn't want to live with this disease either. So, if she wasn't getting healed, maybe she shouldn't live. As she entertained these thoughts, depression and hopelessness seeped into her soul. This is the tipping point to which the enemy wants to bring each person. It wasn't until later in her healing journey that she recognized that this was the spirit of death.

Betrayed by her body, misunderstood by her parents and doctors, and feeling rejected by God, Mia wrestled with helplessness. This is where she made an agreement with this new acquaintance and finally said out loud the message that had been streaming in her head. "Either God will heal me... or I will die." And, because at that time she really believed that she could not be happy unless she was healed, she did not care what happened. This defiant stance—as faulty as it was—empowered her. She no longer felt like a victim.

She wondered how long she would live if she didn't take insulin. Her body was already severely breaking down. Although she drank gallons of water a day and ate continually, she was dehydrated and literally starving.[11] Her clothes were hanging off her body. One of her teachers even asked if she was anorexic. This all compounded the overwhelming shame within her.

This life and death process lasted about six months. Throughout this time her parents continued to plead with her. "Please," they'd beg, "You can do it. It will be okay." Over and over they tried to convince her to listen to the doctors—who told her as long as she monitored her blood sugar she could have a full life.

But Mia couldn't hear this. Agreeing to take insulin was not based on logic. Objectively, she could see that a healthy life was possible, but now being healed by God alone had become the central issue of her heart. She erroneously believed that if she had this disease she really would be deficient. For Mia, it had become a relational issue between her and God. If He didn't come through for her here, could she trust Him to come through for her in other areas? It felt like everything was at stake.

THE SHIFT

There is hope in this story. Mia is alive and well today. However, the journey between this fourteen-year-old's broken life and where she got free was long and hard—which is why she wanted to share her story with you.

She wants you to know that anything that shackles your mind with fear, anger, and shame are from the enemy. Any thoughts that prompt you to live in rebellion or consider death are from the enemy. The enemy will offer these companions to you with the presumption of making your life better, but if you embrace them, they will ultimately taunt and isolate you. And since they are sent by the enemy to destroy your life, there is no good fruit in following them—ever.

---

[11] Mia's body wasn't producing insulin. And without insulin—which is what transports water and nutrients into one's cells—a person cannot get hydrated or process food.

So, how did things turn around? How did Mia come to understand the truth and step out of the faulty mindset that she had taken on? It was through her dad.

One day as she sat in the sun in her backyard, contemplating the unraveling of her life, her dad came out to talk to her. He sat on the grass, put his head down and began to cry—gut-wrenching sobs that actually startled Mia. When he looked at her, his eyes pleaded, *I don't want you to die.* Choking on his words he said, "If you don't begin taking insulin, I don't think you'll live much longer, and I don't want to lose you." And even though she didn't fully understand the link between her dad and God as her Father, she felt a love and care that opened something up within her.

That was it. That was what shifted things for her. Her dad had always been a strong man. Up to this point in her life she didn't know if she'd ever seen him cry. So when she saw her dad's heart breaking, something broke within her. It was then that she agreed to go to the hospital. Things were not resolved for her internally. She still wrestled with why she hadn't physically gotten healed. But, for the first time in months, she opened her heart. She began to see that she could still believe God for healing, even while taking insulin.

STEPPING INTO THE LIGHT

Mia learned that sometimes on the journey of life, you don't have to have everything resolved and figured out. You don't have to understand the "why" or "why not" when you're in the middle of it. Just take the first step into the light and begin to walk. The dark, broken places in your heart will begin to heal when you live in the light[12] of the Father's love.

---

[12] In the natural as well as in the spiritual realm, you will always see things more clearly in the light.

"Then Jesus spoke to them again, saying, 'I am the light of the world. He who follows Me shall not walk in darkness, but have the light of life.'" John 8:12; NKJV

"For once you were full of darkness, but now you have light from the LORD. So live as people of light! For this light within you produces only what is good and right and true... Take no part in the worthless deeds of evil and darkness; instead, expose them. ... evil intentions will be exposed when the light shines on them, for the light makes everything visible."
Ephesians 5:8-9, 11, 13b- 14; NLT

"Today I have given you the choice between life and death, between blessings and curses. Now I call on heaven and earth to witness the choice you make. Oh, that you would choose life, so that you and your descendants might live!" Deuteronomy 30:19; NLT

CHOOSING LIFE

Mia yo-yoed for years between expectantly believing God... and hope deferred. She was finally able to fully choose life when she began to believe how much God loved her. It was His love that allowed her to begin to trust Him even though she didn't understand.

Through her wrestling she finally came to believe that God was not withholding from her.[13] He showed her a powerful principle:
God will not short-circuit His very best in any of our lives to justify, validate, or simply make us happy. He wants us to be mature— whole and powerful in Him.

Are you waiting upon God for healing? Are you believing Him to bring you physical or emotional wholeness? Good. Pursue Him in the

---

[13] "For the LORD God is our sun and our shield. He gives us grace and glory. The LORD will withhold no good thing from those who do what is right." Psalm 84:11; NLT

truth of who He is, and believe. Declare His Word back to Him and stand on His promises.

But if it does not happen immediately, ask God if you are supposed to stand and contend for it or if He has you in a process that is necessary for your holistic wellness. For example, if God had healed Mia's body before He addressed the spiritual/emotional issues of fear, anger, rebellion, shame, and the spirit of death that had an inroad into her life, she would not be whole or free. She would still be living under the destructive influence of the enemy. God wants us all to be whole—spirit, soul, and body.

KEY TO VICTORY

➤ Receive God's love

God's love will heal, align, cover, strengthen, and sustain you—in the deepest, most hurting places of your life, even before your issues are resolved. God's love is not just an idea. It's who He is; it's alive. And it reverberates with power!

One of the biggest points of connection I've found in receiving God's love is that when I embrace it, something happens in my heart that expands my capacity to love Him back. His love draws me to trust Him, even when I don't see how things will work out. His love strengthens me to be able to believe what His Word says. The link between His love and His Word is inseparable—He is literally both. John 1:1 tells us that Jesus is the Word of God; and 1 John 4:7 tells us that He is love.

> "In the beginning was the Word, and the Word was with God, and the Word was God." John 1:1; NKJV

> "Beloved, let us love one another, for love is of God; and everyone who loves is born of God and knows God... God is love." 1 John 4:7, 8b; NKJV

"May you experience the love of Christ, though it is too great to understand fully. Then you will be made complete with all the fullness of life and power that comes from God."
Ephesians 3:19; NLT

"Look with wonder at the depth of the Father's marvelous love that He has lavished on us! He has called us and made us His very own beloved children." 1 John 3:1a; TPT

"For we know how dearly God loves us, because He has given us the Holy Spirit to fill our hearts with His love."
Romans 5:2a, 5b; NLT

Message from God's Heart:

"Oh, My treasured one, if you could see and understand how much I love you, you would be able to rest in the process that is before you.

I have you—in it.

I have you in the palm of My hand and have not forgotten or missed anything you've cried out for.

There are things that you don't understand yet from your current vantage point, but I have you.

Come to Me.

It is My delight to sit with you and hold you.

It is My delight to strengthen and empower you.

It is My delight to heal you and completely restore you.

Let Me give to you what I paid the highest price for you to have.

I know you've tried so hard to attain it.
Remember that it's a gift.
You can't earn it.
You can't work for it.
All you can do is receive it.

'How?' you ask. 'How can I receive it?'
You receive it by receiving Me.
Soak in My tender, overwhelming, everything-given love for you.
Focus on who I am and what I've done for you.

I could not have done one more thing.
I gave it all.
I love you, My child.

As you believe this truth you will be strengthened and empowered to receive everything I've given to you."

5

FINDING FREEDOM

Restoration from Addiction

Have you ever done something—like splurge on ice cream, have a drink, shop, smoke, gamble, or even something hurtful like look at pornography, and realize that doing "that thing" made you feel good for a while? That it literally boosted your mood? And then, the next time you felt down, you were drawn to do that thing again? This is how addictions unconsciously start in people's lives.

If you do that thing again... and again... when you want to feel better, you will create pathways in your brain that reinforce you "needing" that thing. Before I understood the cycle of addiction, I found that when I wanted to boost how I felt I'd bake cookies. Eating sweets gave me an endorphin high, and I found myself craving them often. Sugar became my addiction.

This obviously wasn't healthy, and God began to show me the negative effects this was beginning to have on my life. He let me see that I was using this artificial high to feel good instead of dealing with the root of why I felt sad, lonely, or upset about something. By the time I understood this, the pull of it felt entrapping.

After work, I'd stop and get frozen yogurt with my favorite toppings—almost every day. As I recognized this was becoming a problem I sensed the Lord asking me, "Will you lean on Me and let Me fill you instead of trying to fill yourself?"

It was a process, but as I learned to follow God, He empowered me to choose Him and get free. Now I enjoy sweets periodically, but they are no longer my "go-to" when I want to feel better. If you find yourself bound to anything, or have to hide what you are doing because you know it isn't healthy, God has an answer for you. He wants to empower you to step into freedom.

SETH'S STORY

Seth was raised in an erratic home where he never quite knew what he was going to get. At times, the climate of his home was one of indifference, with very little interaction. But most often, the air was thick with a tension that required him to walk on eggshells. At a young age, he learned the value of being "invisible" so that he could avoid the chaos that was just under the surface.

He always wanted life to be different. He wanted a home with no yelling. No passive aggressive games. No withholding love. In an attempt to push this dysfunction away, Seth mastered living behind the façade of "everything's fine."

He overcompensated for his feelings of disconnection by working hard. He became an ambitious student and an excellent employee. People thought he had it all together, but when difficulties arose, he was very aware that he was lacking substance behind this mask he'd constructed. He felt like a fraud, which created pressure within him.

As this pressure mounted, Seth began to go out at night to let the steam off. It was no big deal at first. He'd get dinner with friends and have a couple of drinks—just to take the edge off. He really liked how he felt not having to hold everything together. Drinking helped him feel a semblance of freedom. He could let go and laugh. And the pressure and anxiety subsided, at least for a bit.

The true impact of Seth's drinking was such a slow progression that he was surprised one night by how desperate he felt when no one could go out with him. Thinking about going home without drinking to alleviate his restlessness startled him. So he swung by the liquor store. He assured himself, *I don't need alcohol. It just helps me relax.*

But this particular night, as he sat at home, alone, he felt the emptiness that he'd been trying to push away his whole life. He got a glimpse of the starkness that permeated his soul, and he didn't like what he saw.

He didn't see a way out, so he opened a bottle and tried to deaden his loneliness with a drink... then another... and another. When he awoke the next morning with a piercing headache, he thought, *What am I doing? This is no way to live. There has got to be more.*

The irony was—because Seth was responsible and worked hard—no one around him knew that he'd begun to crumble on the inside. When he felt lost and out of control, he drank. He did whatever he could to squelch those feelings and relieve his anxiety. Sadly, the more he drank, the more depressed and lonely he became.

In the desperate places of his heart, he cried out, *Is there an answer for me? Life has never felt secure, and people are untrustworthy. What's the point? Life is hard, and most of the time it doesn't make sense.*

Leaning In

One day after work he decided to take a walk at the beach to try to clear his head. As he aimlessly wandered along the sand, he was drawn towards a group of people who were playing guitars and singing around a bonfire. He leaned in, listening. There was something appealing about them, and he felt pulled to the periphery of this group to hear what they were singing about.

Huh. It was Jesus. They were singing to God. Seth hadn't been raised in any kind of religious home—let alone a Christian home. In fact, religion had been mocked, and the need for God was seen as a weakness. But what he felt from this group of people did not seem weak. It felt strong and alive.

Maybe it wasn't a coincidence that he went to that beach that day and saw that particular group. Maybe there was something here for him. Maybe this was a part of his answer. What if God was real? After about an hour of listening to them sing, they all sat down around the fire pit and someone got up to talk.

And, can you believe it? The person sharing talked about living in freedom. He read verses from the Bible like:

> "In my distress I prayed to the LORD,
> and the LORD answered me and set me free." Psalm 118:5; NLT

> "'I speak eternal truth,' Jesus said. 'When you sin you are not free. You've become a slave in bondage to your sin.
> ...So if the Son sets you free from sin, then become a true son and be unquestionably free!'" John 8:34, 36; TPT

Seth was fascinated by what he heard. *Was it possible that God could take away my need to drink?* he wondered. He would be grateful for this, because as "good" as alcohol made him feel in the moment, afterwards he felt an unbearable crushing weight of emptiness—which drew him to drink more.

It was in these times that he was most aware that his life was not working. He hadn't labeled his drinking as "sin," but he had to admit that alcohol had put him into many awkward and compromising situations over the last few years. He had done many things he wished he could erase. He had hurt others; he did have regrets. And he felt shame. But as he listened around the fire that night, he felt a surge of hope.

"And you shall know the truth, and the truth shall make you free." John 8:33; NKJV

"For the law of the Spirit of life in Christ Jesus has made me free from the law of sin and death." Romans 8:2; NKJV

When the guy on the beach finished talking, people casually mingled and chatted together. Several in the group openly welcomed Seth and seemed genuinely happy to meet him. There was lots of laughing as they roasted marshmallows and made s'mores. It was comfortable. It felt safe. This is what he wanted his whole life—to be accepted. They encouraged Seth to stay connected with them. They exchanged phone numbers and invited him to their church.

LIVING FREE

Seth was excited about finally meeting some people who had what he wanted. They had joy and hope. As he began to do things with them, beyond simply going to church, he felt stronger. He honestly still felt the pull of alcohol, but he noticed that when he hung out with people who accepted and cared about him, it was much easier to resist the temptation to drink.

Through the example of his new friends, he got a glimpse of what it looked like to actually be free. As he learned about the price that Jesus paid for him, Seth began to pursue God. He came to see that being free is not just for a privileged few; it's God's provision for everyone.

He began to understand that freedom is more than an idea, a feeling, or a philosophy. It is a state of being. And he wanted it.

GETTING FREE, STAYING FREE

Many people struggle with addiction. That might make sense for those who don't have the power of God in their lives, but why are so many Christian believers stuck? Churches are full of those who "know" the truth of God yet feel helpless over the pull of sin. God shares some tools with us for how to not only *get* free but also *stay* free.

> "... We are no longer slaves to sin. For when we died with Christ we were set free from the power of sin... When He died, He died once to break the power of sin. But now that He lives, He lives for the glory of God. So you also should consider yourselves to be dead to the power of sin and alive to God through Christ Jesus." Romans 6:6b-7, 10-11; NLT

> "No temptation has overtaken you except what is common to mankind. And God is faithful; He will not let you be tempted beyond what you can bear. But when you are tempted, He will also provide a way out so that you can endure it."
> 1 Corinthians 10:13; NIV

> "Therefore submit to God. Resist the devil and he will flee from you. Draw near to God and He will draw near to you. Cleanse your hands, you sinners; and purify your hearts, you double-minded." James 4:7-8; NKJV

> "So I say, walk by the Spirit, and you will not gratify the desires of the flesh. For the flesh desires what is contrary to the Spirit, and the Spirit what is contrary to the flesh. They are in conflict with each other, so that you are not to do whatever you want."
> Galatians 5:16-18; NIV

These powerful verses highlight how you can receive God's freedom in your life. However, as a believer, you likely already know these things. You know that:

- Jesus paid the price to set you free.
- God will provide a way of escape if you draw near to Him and resist the enemy.
- You will not gratify your fleshly desires if you walk with the Holy Spirit.

But if you continue to struggle, I encourage you to glean from Seth's story, remembering what solidified his freedom. He gratefully received what God did for him, but he also found that it was much easier to walk it out with others. Establishing a strong network of friends and mentors became his lifeline. He got into the habit of calling someone whenever he struggled and was tempted to drink.

Key to Victory

➤ Establish healthy relationships

If you're struggling with an addiction, ask God to connect you with people who can walk alongside you. If you—instead of indulging in a counterfeit pleasure—reach out to someone who is committed to your success, it will be much easier to overcome.

> "And one standing alone can be attacked and defeated, but two can stand back-to-back and conquer..." Ecclesiastes 4a:12; TLB

> "And let us consider how we may spur one another on toward love and good deeds, not giving up meeting together... but encouraging one another..." Hebrews 10:24-25; NIV

> "Brothers and sisters, if someone is caught in a sin, you who live by the Spirit should restore that person gently. But watch yourselves,

or you also may be tempted. Carry each other's burdens, and in this way you will fulfill the law of Christ." Galatians 6:1-2; NIV

"Therefore confess your sins to each other and pray for each other so that you may be healed. The prayer of a righteous person is powerful and effective." James 5:16; NIV

Seth understood that stepping out of his addiction was not something he had done on his own—it was through God and others. Having good people to link arms with will strengthen you as you walk out your own life's journey.

Healthy relationships are a powerful God-given resource that will:
- bring connection to your heart;
- challenge you;
- support you;
- encourage you to make healthy choices.

REDEMPTION

As Seth got free, he decided he would do what he could to help others get free. He wanted something good to come from all the lonely years he had experienced. If he could share his story maybe the pain of those years would not be wasted. He was excited to bring God's truth and goodness to others. He especially loved the verse in Romans 8:28 that says, "...God works [all things] for the good of those who love Him, who have been called according to His purpose."

Seeing how God was using his broken past to bring freedom to others gave Seth great purpose. It felt like the sweetest redemption. Likewise, when you receive God's deliverance, He will use the places you've previously been bound in to bring hope and freedom to others as well.

This is His redemptive plan for each of our lives. Genesis 50:20 highlights this principle. What was meant for evil, God will use for good.

And He not only restores us, but He gives increase where we lived in brokenness and shame.

> "Instead of your shame you will receive a double portion,
> and instead of disgrace you will rejoice in your inheritance.
> And so you will inherit a double portion in your land,
> and everlasting joy will be yours." Isaiah 61:7; NIV

Message from God's Heart:

"My child, whom I so greatly cherish,
I have wanted to connect with you your entire life.
I knew the path you'd walk.
I knew the pain you'd experience.
I knew the choices you'd make—good and bad.

You may not have recognized Me in your difficulties,
but when you look back you will see many 'coincidences'
where I intervened in your life.
Can you see how I set things up for you to find Me?

I've always had an incredible plan for you.
    Even in your darkest times,
    even when you wanted to give up and check out,
    even when you felt alone and abandoned, I was there—
calling you to Myself.
I have been seeking you your whole life.

I came to fulfill you.
I came so you could be free.
The more you come to Me and connect with My people,
the stronger and more free you will be.
You will be known as My mighty, overcoming one."

6

CHOOSING LIFE

Rising Above Health Issues

I have personally had many things to overcome. At times, it's been disheartening waiting for my breakthroughs. But as I have pursued God, He has shown me how to rise above my most difficult circumstances. In this chapter I will share a part of my health journey and how God has walked—and is walking—with me through it.

It is possible to overcome, regardless of what's going on in your life. I want to share my own story with you to impart what I have learned and show you how to use the keys God has revealed to me. I pray you can glean from them as you step into your own victory.

MY STORY

When I was in my late twenties, I began to have joint issues that caused me a great deal of pain and inflammation. I went to the doctor, got blood work done, and the results showed that I had rheumatoid arthritis. This threw me for a loop as no one in my family had RA. Believing God for the provision of His healing, I began to pursue Him for answers.

As the years passed and the pain worsened, I went to the doctor to see if there was a solution that would bring relief to me. The doctor wanted me to take a type of oral chemotherapy to suppress my body from attacking itself. The medicine, however, was very strong and would have required me to be on two forms of birth control because it could cause birth defects. My husband and I—who had only been married for a short time and wanted children—were not comfortable with the potential consequences of this, so I did not take the medication. The result of this choice was chronic pain—for years. Every step hurt. Every movement cost me. As I cried out to the Lord and sought Him for healing, I learned to live with the pain, but questions were rising in my heart.

I had a full-time job that was becoming more and more difficult to do. I was extremely thin and had very little energy. Finally, I went to the doctor again and asked if I could get a note to take some time off of work so I could rest and heal. I thought two weeks would be a good amount of time.

She had me do more blood work and told me to take six weeks off, which concerned me regarding the seriousness of my situation. A couple of days later, I took a nap and woke up with the words "Urgent Care" flashing in my mind's eye. I felt like God was prompting me to go in and get seen right away. I went to the Emergency Room, and they immediately admitted me into the hospital.

They drew countless vials of blood, did numerous cultures and biopsies, and ran a multitude of tests but still could not assess what was going on with my body. As I lay in that hospital bed crying out to God, I began to struggle with hopelessness. Even the specialists could not find an answer, and things were getting worse. I was in a great deal of pain, and although I didn't know it at that point, my body had begun to shut down.

I don't remember anything after that until I "woke up" in ICU on a ventilator. I had no idea what had happened. I didn't know how much time had passed. I didn't know what was wrong with my body. I felt stuck and totally helpless as my arms were even tied down—so I wouldn't pull the ventilation tube out of my mouth. Was this going to be how I lived the rest of my life? I didn't know. Fear tried to grip my heart.

I asked God, "Are You taking me Home?" I felt like He said, "No. You have not fulfilled your destiny yet, but you need to choose life." At this point where I could not even talk, I knew that choosing life had to do with my mindset. It had to do with making a choice to say "yes" to God and "yes" to life—which meant I had to guard my mind from fear and the voice of the enemy.

I remembered phrases from a verse in Deuteronomy 30:19-20,
> "...I have set before you life and death... choose life... love the LORD your God... obey His voice... cling to Him, for He is your life and the length of your days..."

So I chose life by saying in my mind, "I choose life. Jesus, I choose You. I love You. You are my life. You are the length of my days..."

I began to recite any verses I had memorized over the years, and I made them personal.

> Lord, You are my shepherd... Psalm 23:1
> God, You love the world... You love *me*... John 3:16
> Lord, You are my rock, and fortress, and deliverer.... Psalm 18:1
> Lord, You are great and mighty in power... Psalm 147:5
> Jesus, by Your stripes I am healed... Isaiah 53:5

Whatever I could remember, I began to meditate on.

EXALTING THE NAME OF THE LORD

God prompted me to recall the power of His name and His attributes. He reminded me how He revealed Himself in His Word. He showed me how His name would give me access to tap into that part of Him. If I needed:

- deliverance, I could pull on Him as my Deliverer;
- healing, I could pull on Him as my Healer;
- comfort, I could pull on Him as my Comforter;
- hope, I could pull on Him as my Hope;
- peace, I could pull on Him as my Peace.

I began to recount the names of God.

"Lord, You are the Captain of the Hosts; the Ancient of Days;
my Abba Father; the Prince of Peace. You are my King;
the Eternal One; the Merciful One who's enthroned in the heavens;
my Justice; the Lion of the Tribe of Judah.
You are my Strong Tower; the Rock of Ages;
the Creator of all things; my Redeemer; my Savior.
You are the Sun of Righteousness with healing in Your wings.
You are my Hope; the Lover of my soul..."

I would meditate on His names until they resonated within me. As I did this His presence embraced me. It was like He was wrapping Himself around me as He infilled me. Declaring God's names and promises ushered me into a place of worship that transformed me.

"The name of the LORD is a strong tower;
The righteous run to it and are safe." Proverbs 18:10; NKJV

"...[W]e will walk in the name of the LORD our God forever and ever." Micah 4:5b; NKJV

"And He has enough treasures to lavish generously upon all who call on Him. And it's true: 'Everyone who calls on the name of the LORD Yahweh will be rescued and experience new life.'"
Romans 10:12b-13; TPT

MY RECOVERY

It was a long journey to recover. They found that I had systemic lupus erythematosis. My kidneys had completely shut down, and I'd gotten sepsis. I was shocked to find that I'd gained seventy pounds of fluid in one week from total renal failure and had been undergoing dialysis while I was unconscious. They also began chemotherapy to try to stop my body from attacking itself.

I had lost my ability to stand and walk. I couldn't even bend my own legs and scoot myself up in bed. I had to choose every day to say "yes" to Him as I leaned in to believe the promises of His Word... or I would have given up.

I remember thinking, *Will I be able to stand again so I can use the bathroom by myself?* Relearning how to walk felt like the hardest thing I had ever done. This was likely because at that time my bone marrow was not producing red blood cells the way it was supposed to, so anything that required strength was difficult to do.

And although God did bring a measure of supernatural healing to me, it was interesting that He also chose to use doctors and medicine in my recovery. He specifically used my nephrologist. Before I went into ICU, I had a kidney biopsy, which typically takes four days to get back the results. My doctor, who knew my kidneys were not functioning said, "She's not going to live that long." So he had someone drive my biopsy to Cedars-Sinai Medical Center in Los Angeles and bring the results back so I could start dialysis immediately. That saved my life.

What a beautiful provision. God could have supernaturally touched my kidneys so they perfectly functioned. But, at that time, He didn't. Why? I don't know.

- Maybe someone saw the testimony of Jesus in me—as I shared Him often with those in the hospital.
- Maybe He was doing something in those around me who walked this journey with me.
- Maybe He was building something in me that I would not have developed if He'd given me the quick miracle for which I was praying.

I don't know, but as I focused on God—in my questions and uncertainty—His grace and mercy covered me.

I do not want to spend much time on the specific health issues I walked through—as the purpose of this book is not to focus on the difficulties but to release the heart and victory of the Lord through them. However, I do want to share enough of my story so that when I talk about how it's possible to overcome, regardless of what you're facing, you know I've been through the tough places. I am not writing this book as theory. I have lived the keys that I will share with you, that sustained my life and brought me hope.

The testimony of my life is God's sustaining grace. Look what He's brought me through. In the last seven years I:

- spent sixty-nine days in the hospital;
- underwent nine treatments of chemotherapy;
- had six surgeries (including a total knee replacement and a total elbow replacement);
- got a bone infection from the elbow replacement—which required two revision surgeries;
- had a pic line with very strong IV antibiotics to get rid of the bone infection, which gave me horribly negative side effects that were worse than the chemo;

• began taking an immune suppressor to help my body not attack itself, and I consequently got Shingles when my white blood count dropped significantly;

• had many blood sugar issues from being on high doses of prednisone.

I have been discouraged. I have gotten weary. The enemy has tried to steal my dignity and mock how I look, from the negative effects of the Lupus and the medication—which caused rashes, blisters, mouth sores, inflammation, a puffy face, dark circles under my eyes, and hair loss. It has been exceedingly hard, but God has walked with me.

Regardless of how things look in the natural, He continues to call me to believe the promises of His Word. God's heart is to restore, prosper, heal, and redeem each of us.

"Beloved, I pray that you may prosper in all things and be in health, just as your soul prospers." 3 John 1:2; NKJV

"God is our refuge and strength,
an ever-present help in trouble.
Therefore we will not fear..." Psalm 46:1-2a; NIV

"...Forget not all His benefits:
Who forgives all your iniquities,
Who heals all your diseases,
Who redeems your life from destruction,
Who crowns you with lovingkindness and tender mercies."
Psalm 103:2b-4; NKJV

"'He Himself bore our sins' in His body on the cross, so that we might die to sins and live for righteousness; 'by His wounds you have been healed.'" 1 Peter 2:24; NIV

God's heart is one of blessing. He wants you to:

- prosper and be in good health;
- enjoy the benefits of His forgiveness, healing, and redemption;
- live your life "on earth as it is in heaven" Matthew 6:10. (And there is no sickness, disease, or hopelessness in heaven).

So what do you do when you believe God's Word but do not see things in your life aligning to His promises? What then? How do you navigate that? What do you do when you believe God yet your natural circumstances are not changing for the better?

OVERWHELMED

I remember one critical time I was in the hospital fighting the bone infection in my arm. I was having very high fevers and was in a lot of pain. The pain was so intense that I was considering telling the doctor to just cut my arm off so I wouldn't have to continue taking the antibiotics that were wreaking havoc in my body. I know that sounds foolish and shortsighted, but things were that bad.

As I struggled, I saw the Lord in my mind's eye shaking His head, to say "no." And in my spirit I could hear Him say,
"Do not entertain that thought.
Do not even put it out there as an option.
That thought is from the enemy and is not My will for you.
Do not agree with him.
Do not give voice to what he's whispering to you."

Once I heard God's heart for me, I could agree with *Him* and declare, "I will keep my arm. I will have a full recovery. I speak health and wholeness over my body." But until I disciplined my mind, I cannot tell you how many times that thought crossed my mind. Over and over I had to refuse it.

"For the weapons of our warfare are not of the flesh, but divinely powerful... We are destroying speculations and every lofty thing raised up against the knowledge of God, and we are *taking every thought captive to the obedience of Christ.*" 2 Corinthians 10:4a, 5; NASB; italics added

As I pushed back the enemy and agreed with God, I felt His power and pleasure pour into me. This strengthened me. As I lifted Him above my circumstances, His goodness and songs of deliverance rose up within me.

THE POWER OF WORSHIP

I got caught up in His presence that day and began to worship Him.
I declared the greatness of His name.
I sang to Him in my hospital bed.
I sang in the Spirit.
I got lost in the wonder of His presence and power.
I felt so embraced by Him that I was startled when someone came into my room and asked if I was okay.

I don't know how long or how loud I was singing. I just know that that afternoon everything shifted for me. I went from feeling frustrated and helpless to being empowered by the living God. Even though *nothing* looked different in the natural, *everything* looked different in the Spirit. Exalting Him above what I was going through allowed me to see from His perspective. It aligned me to Him.

When God calls you to Himself and fills you with His truth and mercy, you will be drawn to worship Him. As you connect with Him, you will experience His love. A song or words of affection will begin to rise up within you. It's not about music, skill, or gifting. It's simply an authentic expression of delight that *He* rises up within you.

Worship is the truest, most powerful thing you can do in life. And because it is an issue of the heart, it requires you to be honest with how you feel. Cry out to God when you're struggling. We see in the Psalms that this is what King David did. Over and over he poured out his heart to God, and as he did, his heart turned to worship. Worship changed how he saw things; it will change how you see things too.

> "I cry out to the LORD...
> I pour out my complaint before Him;
> I declare before Him my trouble.
> When my spirit was overwhelmed within me...
> I cried out to You, O LORD...
> Bring my soul out of prison, that I may praise Your name..."
> Psalm 142:1a-3a, 5a, 7a; NKJV

> "Day and night I have only tears for food,
> while my enemies continually taunt me, saying,
> 'Where is this God of yours?'
> My heart is breaking...
> Why am I discouraged?
> Why is my heart so sad?
> I will put my hope in God!
> I will praise Him again—
> my Savior and my God!" Psalm 42:3-4a, 5; NLT

> "Stand in awe of Him...
> For He has not despised my cries of deep despair.
> He's my first responder to my sufferings,
> and He didn't look the other way when I was in pain.
> He was there all the time, listening to the song of the afflicted.
> You're the reason for my praise; it comes from You and goes to You...
> Bring Yahweh praise and you will find Him.
> Your hearts will overflow with life forever!"
> Psalm 22:23b, 24-25a, 26b; TPT

🔑 KEY TO VICTORY

In this chapter I will share two keys that have personally become life-lines when I find myself in a desperate place. I will share them both here, because they have been foundational to my victory and because of the multiplied effect they have when utilized with each other. Together these keys are exponentially powerful.

🔑 CHAPTER'S 1ST KEY

➤ **Worship God**

Above all things, worship connects you to God. He will come to you. He will wrap Himself around you, well up within you, and literally indwell you. He will inhabit you as you praise Him.

> "But You are holy, You who inhabit the praises of Israel."
> Psalm 22:3; NHEB

> "I will sing to the LORD,
> For He has triumphed gloriously...
> The LORD is my strength and song,
> And He has become my salvation;
> He is my God, and I will praise Him;
> My father's God, and I will exalt Him." Exodus 15:1a-2; NKJV

> "I will bless the LORD at all times;
> His praise shall continually be in my mouth.
> My soul shall make its boast in the LORD...
> Oh, magnify the LORD with me,
> And let us exalt His name together.
> I sought the LORD, and He heard me,
> And delivered me from all my fears...
> The angel of the LORD encamps all around those who fear Him,

And delivers them." Psalm 34:1-2a, 4, 7; NKJV

"Worship the LORD with gladness.
Come before Him, singing with joy.
Acknowledge that the LORD is God!
...Enter His gates with thanksgiving;
go into His courts with praise.
Give thanks to Him and praise His name.
For the LORD is good.
His unfailing love continues forever,
and His faithfulness continues to each generation."
Psalm 100:2-3a, 4-5; NLT

Worship will naturally flow from you when you remember who God is and declare the truth back to Him. It positions you to see from God's perspective and rise above your circumstances.

CHAPTER'S 2ND KEY

➢ Pray in the Spirit

The second key is praying in the Spirit—which is a benefit you can have when you get baptized by the Holy Spirit. What does it mean to be baptized by the Holy Spirit? First of all, *receiving* the Holy Spirit happens when you get saved. Every believer is filled with the Spirit of God when they accept Jesus.

"Repent and be baptized, every one of you, in the name of Jesus Christ for the forgiveness of your sins. And you will receive the gift of the Holy Spirit." Acts 2:38; NIV

"The Spirit of God, who raised Jesus from the dead, *lives in you...*"
Romans 8:11a; NLT; italics added

"Do you not know that you are the temple of God and that the

Spirit of God *dwells in you?"* 1 Corinthians 3:16; NKJV;
italics added

When you get saved the Holy Spirit fills you. This allows you to enjoy
God's presence, hear His voice, and understand His Word. It's wonderful to be *filled* with His Spirit. But there's more! There is a "second"
baptism that Matthew 3:11 describes where Jesus came to "baptize
you with the Holy Spirit and fire." Being baptized with Holy the Spirit
empowers you. This baptism gives you access to a spiritual language—
which is called "praying in the Spirit" or "tongues."[15]

We will discuss the benefits of this gift and how to receive it, but first I
want to address why there has been so much resistance to it. The resistance is from satan, who strategically works to divide the church. Of
all of the Holy Spirit's gifts, the enemy has targeted this one because he
knows there is supernatural power released as you connect with God
in the language of His Spirit.

There's no reason to shy away from this spiritual gift of tongues. It is
given by God. Everything God gives is good.

"Every good and perfect gift is from above, coming down from the
Father of the heavenly lights..." James 1:17a; NIV

THE BENEFITS

One of the greatest benefits I've found for praying in the Spirit is that
God literally prays His heart through you. That is profound. When
you pray in tongues you are praying God's perfect will. And His

---

[15] The Greek word used for "tongue" in the New Testament is glossa. This is the same word used
many other times in Scripture (such as in James 1:26, 3:5-6, 8; 1 Peter 3:10; 1 John 3:18) where
"tongue" simply refers to speech, or a language/dialect. www.blueletter.org
What makes tongues/praying in the Spirit different than just speaking is the supernatural
component of how God can speak through someone when they get baptized by His Spirit and
receive a spiritual language. This language is often referred to simply as "tongues."

prayers always hit the mark to accomplish His purposes! This is especially helpful when:

- you don't know what God's will is in a particular situation;
- you have prayed and prayed and your answer has not come;
- you feel stuck, weary, and overwhelmed.

"But if we hope for what we do not yet have, we wait for it patiently. In the same way, the Spirit helps us in our weakness. We do not know what we ought to pray for, but the Spirit himself intercedes for us through wordless groans. And He who searches our hearts knows the mind of the Spirit, because the Spirit intercedes for God's people in accordance with the will of God."
Romans 8:25-27; NIV

As the Spirit prays His heart through you, you will be personally encouraged and empowered. Praying in the Spirit will:

- strengthen your connection with God;
- increase your anointing;[16]
- usher you into God's will;
- give you understanding in things you didn't previously know.

Whenever I feel stuck, I pray in tongues until I have understanding. For example, there were times when I was writing this book that I had a concept in my heart that I was struggling to articulate. In those moments, I would stop and pray in the Spirit. I asked God to release His wording, wisdom, and anointing. It was not always immediate, but as I connected with Him and prayed, a new idea would come to my mind. He would show me how to say what He wanted to say. Over and over again, God brought clarity to me when I needed it.

---

[16] Anointing refers to being set apart for a specific purpose. God anointed Jesus. As believers we are also anointed to accomplish God's Kingdom purposes—preaching good news, healing the brokenhearted, proclaiming liberty to the captives... Isaiah 61. Praying in your spiritual language will empower you to more effectively do all that He's called you to do.

I also pray in tongues when I am:
- worshipping;
- needing breakthrough;
- doing spiritual warfare;
- interceding for others.

I love knowing that I am not only connecting with God but I'm also partnering with Him to pray His exact will.

MY EXPERIENCE

I was young—in sixth or seventh grade—when I began to pursue God for this gift. I went to a church service that gave an invitation to come up and receive a spiritual language. I wanted all that God had for me but was uncertain about how to do it. The person ministering to me said, "Just start making sounds and your language will come."

I responded, "I don't know what to say."

She said, "Just open your mouth." So I opened my mouth.
She chuckled and said, "You need to use your own vocal cords to speak."

But... I didn't know what to say. I didn't speak in tongues that night because I didn't want to make anything up. I felt frustrated, as I didn't know how to receive it. Finally, one morning at church, when we were corporately in a strong flow of worship, something released like a floodgate within me. I began to pray and sing in a spiritual language that flowed through me like a river. God's glory and wonder filled me as this happened.

Praying in tongues will empower you greatly.

Do you have a spiritual language? Would you like one? If you would, ask God for it. And remember that just like all of His gifts, it is free.

You cannot earn it; you just have to receive it.

> "And when He had said this, He breathed on them and said to them, 'Receive the Holy Spirit.'" John 20:22; NKJV

PRAYER TO RECEIVE

There's no set way to receive a gift. There's no formula. Like everything with God, it's all about relationship. In faith pray something like this:

> "Lord, I ask for this connection with You. I ask You to baptize me with Your Holy Spirit and fire.[17] I want to know the mysteries of Your Spirit. I ask You to give me the gift of tongues so You can pray Your perfect will through my life. Please show me how to receive this gift, and let it become a sweet place of worship and effective intercession we have together. Holy Spirit, I want to know You more. I want to learn how to fully love and connect with You. I love You and Your gifts, and I boldly ask for this one today. Thank You, my God."

Receiving the gift of tongues during worship was my personal experience, and worship often opens up the floodgates of heaven for others as well. Worship releases the flow of the Spirit that makes speaking in tongues easy to access. The main thing is connecting with God as you pursue all that He has for you.

I pray that these two keys—worship and praying in the Spirit—become second nature to you and that through them you find your victory.

---

[17] John the Baptist announced, "I indeed baptize you with water unto repentance, but He who is coming after me is mightier than I, whose sandals I am not worthy to carry. He will baptize you with the Holy Spirit and fire." Matthew 3:11; NKJV

MESSAGE FROM GOD'S HEART:

"Oh, My beloved one, I only have good for you.
I only have great joy, delight, and abundance for you.
I will lead you as you walk with Me.
I will bring life to you.
I have treasures and secrets to share with you.
I will reveal them as we connect.

Come to Me and enjoy the adventure of life
that I have prepared for you.
    I am wonder.
    I am beauty.
    I am the fullness of joy.
And I have all that concerns you.

If you ever begin to doubt that I am working for your good,
know that the enemy is simply trying to discourage you.
Don't let him.
Draw near to Me.
Worship Me.

Let's sing together.
Let's laugh.
Let's delight in each other.
I know it's beyond your understanding, but I am overwhelmed
with love for you.

Come, enjoy Me as I enjoy you, My sweet, sweet love."

7

STANDING

In Faith and Surrender

Ⓦe have looked at a number of powerful keys that can help you overcome the difficulties you face. These keys are tried and true, and when you apply them to your life you will find God's hope and strength increasing in you. However, there may be times when you do everything you know to do and your circumstances still don't change.

OUR VICTORIOUS STORY

God has written His very own story within us, individually and collectively. He has placed you as the main character in a beautiful narrative that is your life. There will be many wonderful things that happen, but just like with any engaging story there will be conflicts to overcome. You will have struggles to rise above. These difficulties are actually intentional. They are the very things that will strengthen and mature you and allow people to see the wonder and power of God through you.

God has an extraordinary plan for your life and wants you to wildly succeed. He's given you access to the resources of heaven so that you can find victory in the midst of the conflicts you face.

So what do you do when you have done everything you know to overcome? You've utilized every means you have? You've knocked on every door... and yet you cannot find a solution to your problem? What do you do when the answers to your beseeching prayers seem to fall flat and you feel stuck?

What does God tell us to do? He tells us to stand. Standing in Him is the most secure, victorious place you can live. God will strengthen and establish you as you stand.

> "Finally, my brethren, be strong in the LORD and in the power of His might.
> ... and having done all, to stand. Stand therefore... "
> Ephesians 6:10, 13b-14a; NKJV

STAND THEREFORE

What does it mean "to stand"? Standing is:
- refusing to waver and give up;
- being rooted;
- taking the position, "I may not understand, but I will not be moved. I will not be shaken, because the Almighty is for me."

> "I have set the LORD always before me;
> Because He is at my right hand I shall not be moved.
> Therefore my heart is glad, and my glory rejoices..."
> Psalm 16:8-9a; NKJV

> "Yes, my soul, find rest in God;
> my hope comes from Him.
> Truly He is my rock and my salvation;

He is my fortress, I will not be shaken." Psalm 62:5-6; NIV

"Cast your cares on the LORD and He will sustain you;
He will never let the righteous be shaken." Psalm 55:22; NIV

Standing is a mindset. It's something you must intentionally choose to do. It's not natural or easy, but God will uphold you as you commit to it. Standing with Him will position you to rise above what you're facing.

"So do not fear, for I am with you; do not be dismayed, for I am your God. I will strengthen you and help you; I will uphold you with my righteous right hand." Isaiah 41:10; NIV

"Yet in all these things we are more than conquerors through Him who loved us." Romans 8:37; NKJV

Standing is vital, but what does it look like to stand when you:
• have overdue bills;
• are struggling with illness;
• lose your job;
• have a broken heart?

We will look at two different ways that God calls us to stand: in faith and surrender. Living in both of these truths simultaneously is not only possible but necessary if you want to access all that God has for you. In the first part of Hebrews 11:33-40, we see a picture of those who stood in faith; the second part shows us those who also learned to stand in surrender.

"[They] who through faith subdued kingdoms, worked righteousness, obtained promises, stopped the mouths of lions, quenched the violence of fire, escaped the edge of the sword, out of weakness were made strong, became valiant in battle, turned to flight the armies of the aliens. Women received their dead raised to life again." Hebrews 11:33-35a; NKJV

"Others were tortured, not accepting deliverance, that they might obtain a better resurrection. Still others had trial of mockings and scourgings, yes, and of chains and imprisonment. They were stoned, they were sawn in two, were tempted, were slain with the sword. They wandered about in sheepskins and goatskins, being destitute, afflicted, tormented—of whom the world was not worthy. They wandered in deserts and mountains, in dens and caves of the earth. And all these, having obtained a good testimony through faith, did not receive the promise, God having provided something better for us, that they should not be made perfect apart from us." Hebrews 11:35b-40; NKJV

As challenging as the second part of this Scripture is, we see that these mighty ones—who also lived in faith—surrendered their lives as they learned to trust God. And even though they didn't receive their promise in the natural, they attained a good testimony. Let's look at the value of both faith and surrender.

STANDING IN FAITH

Standing in faith is living above what you see in the natural. 2 Corinthians 5:7 calls us to "live by faith, not by sight." Faith is a key component in being able to stand. And faith is also how you please God.[18] It's powerful and necessary as you develop your relationship with Him.

Hebrews 11 tells us that faith:
- pleases God;
- gives you an inheritance;
- obeys God;

---

[18] "But without faith it is impossible to please Him, for he who comes to God must believe that He is, and that He is a rewarder of those who diligently seek Him." Hebrews 11:6; NKJV

- strengthens you;
- releases blessing;
- allows you to see into the invisible realm;
- obtains promises;
- overcomes impossibilities;
- brings life to broken, hopeless places.

When you stand in faith—in the face of lack, sickness, questions, and uncertainties—you can be assured that God is in your midst. Faith will usher you into His will and position you to receive that for which you are contending.

> "Jesus said to him, 'If you can believe, all things are possible to him who believes.'" Mark 9:23; NKJV

> "For whatever is born of God overcomes the world. And this is the victory that has overcome the world—our faith.
> ...Now this is the confidence that we have in Him, that if we ask anything according to His will, He hears us. And if we know that He hears us, whatever we ask, we know that we have the petitions that we have asked of Him." 1 John 5:4, 14-15; NKJV

> "So Jesus answered and said to them, 'Have faith in God. For assuredly, I say to you, whoever says to this mountain [your problem], "Be removed and be cast into the sea," and does not doubt in his heart, but believes that those things he says will be done, he will have whatever he says. Therefore I say to you, whatever things you ask when you pray, believe that you receive them, and you will have them.'" Mark 11:22-24; NKJV

Faith opens the door for you to live in the supernatural realm where God reigns and His provision abounds. Faith is what renews your mind and allows you to see things that you previously could not see or understand. Faith allows you to speak to your problem (the mountain before you) and take authority over it.

Standing in faith is vital, but you have likely noticed that not everything you believe for happens in your time frame—when and how you want it. What do you do when you find yourself here? When you declare God's Word over your situation and nothing appears to be happening? This is where we must each learn to embrace the other end of the "standing" spectrum: surrender.

STANDING IN SURRENDER

What does it mean to stand in surrender? This is a tender, powerful place where you choose to trust God with all that is in your heart. It's coming to a place of rest in Him. It's where you remember who He is and how much He loves you.

This kind of surrender is not a place of concession where you abandon your hopes and dreams. No! It is the most courageous of places that requires you to exercise your highest level of faith.

- It's giving Him your understanding when things don't make sense.
- It's the holiest of places where you both believe Him for your dreams fulfilled and where you offer them back to Him.

Let's look at the last part of Hebrews 11 again.

> "Others were tortured... had trial of mockings and scourgings... chains and imprisonment. They were stoned... sawn in two... tempted... slain with the sword. They wandered about... destitute, afflicted, tormented—of whom the world was not worthy... And all these, having obtained a good testimony through faith, did not receive the promise..." Hebrews 11:35b-40; NKJV

They went through incredible atrocities and yet were able to maintain their faith and a good testimony.[19] How? How did they do it and not lose heart? I believe they found a place where God's presence sustained them—which released His supernatural grace and strength into their lives. He will do the same for you. It is here in the secret place that all of this happens.

"He who dwells in the secret place of the Most High
Shall abide under the shadow of the Almighty.
I will say of the LORD, 'He is my refuge and my fortress;
My God, in Him I will trust.'" Psalm 91:1-2; NKJV

"Wait on the LORD;
Be of good courage,
And He shall strengthen your heart;
Wait, I say, on the LORD!" Psalm 27:14; NKJV

"Therefore we do not lose heart. Even though our outward man is perishing, yet the inward man is being renewed day by day. For our light affliction, which is but for a moment, is working for us a far more exceeding and eternal weight of glory, while we do not look at the things which are seen, but at the things which are not seen. For the things which are seen are temporary, but the things which are not seen are eternal." 2 Corinthians 4:16-18; NKJV

As we have seen the necessity of standing in both faith and surrender, there is one important thing we need to ask: How do we *practically* do it? Below, there is a challenging verse that answers this question. We all have access to a powerful key that shows us how to overcome when things are desperate and we don't see a way out.

---

[19] "A good testimony" in the New Testament is translated martyreo, from which we get our word martyr. It means to have a good report; to be a witness; to affirm that one has seen, heard, or experienced something that he knows because it was taught by divine revelation. www.blueletter.org
I believe these surrendered ones—who obtained a good testimony through faith—received divine revelation from God in the midst of their pain, which empowered them to overcome.

"Even though the fig trees have no blossoms,
and there are no grapes on the vines;
even though the olive crop fails,
and the fields lie empty and barren;
even though the flocks die in the fields,
and the cattle barns are empty,
yet I will rejoice in the LORD!
I will be joyful in the God of my salvation!
The Sovereign LORD is my strength!" Habakkuk 3:17-19a; NLT,
italics added

Habakkuk 3:17 describes a dire situation. There was incredible loss of provision and life. It looked like they had no hope, no harvest, and no future. But the answer Habakkuk found in God was to *rejoice*. He went from looking at his circumstances to looking at God. Setting your heart on God will give you hope and bring strength to you. Initially this may not be easy, but the more you do it, the more natural it will become.

Habakkuk acknowledges the devastating reality they are facing. But he makes a volitional choice to rejoice in the Lord in the midst of it. He chooses to trust God's sovereignty. We always have a choice when we feel helpless and things look hopeless. What will you choose?

• You can stand... or lie down and give up.

• You can trust Him and surrender... or get frustrated and "kick against the goads."[20]

• You can delight in God and rejoice... or get disappointed, angry, or resentful.

Choosing to be joyful will shift your perspective and allow you to see

---

[20] Acts 26:14 tells us how Saul resisted God before his conversion. He was "kicking against the goads" doing what he thought was right.

from God's vantage point. Joy will empower you to stand in faith and surrender. It is both the means to being able to stand and the result of your standing. And when you rejoice—even when you don't feel like it—God will fill you with *His* joy and strength.

"The joy of the LORD is your strength." Nehemiah 8:10b; ESV

KEY TO VICTORY

➤ Rejoice

Rejoicing is so powerful, because joy is foundational in God's Kingdom. Romans 14:17 tells us that, "The Kingdom of God is... righteousness, peace, and joy in the Holy Spirit."

Another reason joy is powerful is: Because the enemy has no access to joy, you can defeat him with it. He hates joy. It's so contrary to his nature that it's one of your best weapons in overcoming his attacks. Just like the children of Israel—who shouted in triumph at Jericho and broke through enemy walls—you too can find breakthrough by shouting in triumph. Joy will crumble walls before you and make the enemy small in your life. Rejoicing will exalt God and attract the angelic host around you as you praise the Lord.

> "Praise Him, all His angels!
> Praise Him, all the armies of heaven!
> ...young men and young women, old men and children.
> Let them all praise the name of the Lord.
> For His name is very great..." Psalm 148:2, 12-13a; NLT

Since the enemy cannot rise above joy, his biggest strategy is to keep it far from you. He wants you to focus on what isn't working. However, when you choose joy, God's presence will encompass you—and that changes everything.

"You will show me the path of life;
In Your presence is fullness of joy;
At Your right hand are pleasures forevermore."
Psalm 16:11; NKJV

"My fellow believers, when it seems as though you are facing nothing but difficulties see it as an invaluable opportunity to experience the greatest joy that you can! For you know that when your faith is tested it stirs up power within you to endure all things. And then as your endurance grows even stronger it will release perfection into every part of your being until there is nothing missing and nothing lacking." James 1:2-4; TPT

"When anxiety was great within me,
your consolation brought me joy." Psalm 94:19; NIV

"But let the godly rejoice.
Let them be glad in God's presence.
Let them be filled with joy.
Sing praises to God and to His name!
...His name is the Lord—
rejoice in his presence!" Psalm 68:3-4; NLT

"Rejoice in the LORD always. Again I will say, rejoice!"
Philippians 4:4; NKJV

Joy is dynamic. It's a choice that requires discipline at times; but like Habakkuk, you can choose it regardless of what you're facing. Rejoicing will shift your perspective. It will:
   • give you hope in your weariness;
   • open up the places within you that have been shut down by disappointment;
   • give you a lightness of heart that empowers you to rise above your circumstances.

GETTING PRACTICAL

That's invaluable, but how do you rejoice when you're in a tough place? I have found two practical things you can do that work every single time. That sounds like a bold claim. What could move you from disappointment to joy one-hundred percent of the time?

First, it's turning from looking at your problem to looking at God. It initially takes some discipline to focus on Him in the midst of challenging circumstances. However, if you spend time declaring the names and attributes of God, His Spirit will begin to fill you with the fullness of Himself.[21] The result of this is a confident joy that will flow from you.

One practical thing I did to access joy was compile a list that describes God—so I'd have it at my fingertips when I needed to tap into His character quickly. I organized His names by making a section for each letter of the alphabet. So I have an "A" section, a "B" section, a "C" section…

For example, under the "A" attributes of God, I have:
  Anointed One
  Alpha & Omega
  Abba Father
  Ancient of Days
  Altogether Lovely
  Answers prayer
  Almighty…

Under "B" I have:
  Bright and Morning Star

---

[21] We looked at this in chapter 6 under the "Exalting the Name of the LORD" section; but we're going to revisit it here because it's such an instrumental part of being able to choose joy when things are difficult.

Beautiful
my Banner
Bold
Bountiful
my Breastplate
Blesses us & is Blessed forever...

Under "C" I have:
Captain of the Hosts
Cornerstone
Christ
Creator of the ends of the earth
Courageous
Compassionate
Comforter
Covenant God
Consuming Fire...

As you do this you will be strengthened to believe that God *will* come through for you. The more you know who He is, the more empowered you will be to "consider it all joy" when you go through difficult times. He really is everything you need to overcome.

> "His divine power has given us everything we need for a godly life through our knowledge of Him who called us by His own glory and goodness. 1Peter 1:3; NIV

The *second* practical thing you can do to foster joy in your life is to find something—anything—for which you are thankful. Then focus on that instead of what is difficult.

I have found when I speak out loud the things I am thankful for— spiritual things, relational things, and practical things—joy naturally wells up in my heart.

When I give thanks for my salvation, family, friendships, great weather, good food, health, nature, and my sweet kitty, etc., it is much easier to see what is good in my life and rejoice.

My heart also rejoices when I remember what God has done for me. When I focus on how He has redeemed me—from sin, fear, doubt, shame, anxiety, and emptiness—thankfulness fills my heart, and I can rejoice regardless of what else is going on in my life.

Being thankful:
- will flow joy through your heart;
- allow you to see beyond your problem;
- restore your perspective;
- renew your trust in God.

"Oh, give thanks to the Lord, for He is good!
For His mercy endures forever." Psalm 107:1; NKJV

"Be thankful in all circumstances, for this is God's will for you who belong to Christ Jesus." 1 Thessalonians 5:18; NLT

"Be anxious for nothing, but in everything by prayer and supplication, with thanksgiving, let your requests be made known to God." Philippians 4:6; NKJV

"...Put on love... let the peace of God rule in your hearts... and be thankful." Colossians 3:14a, 15; NKJV

"Always giving thanks to God the Father for everything, in the name of our Lord Jesus Christ." Ephesians 5:20; NIV

MESSAGE FROM GOD'S HEART:

"You have been on an incredible journey, My child.
I know it's been a long road, but I declare today that you are an overcomer and you have everything you need to live in the fullness of Me.

I have both equipped you to stand and empowered you to surrender.
All you have to do is look to Me and follow My lead.

> I am your greatest resource.
> I am your biggest advocate.
> I am your life and hope and the length of your days.

You can have as much of Me as you want.
And because I am infinite, when you're tucked in to Me you have an unlimited well of resources.

In fact, I have treasures uniquely reserved for you.
There are treasures that I have not revealed to anyone else that are for you to discover and share...
secret things that you will find as you dwell with Me.

You have everything you need to:
> defeat the enemy,
> live in My fullness,
> and declare My goodness to the world around you.

Go in My truth and you will prosper and flourish in every way, My love."

8

GOOD PLEASURE

Living in God's Delight

Throughout your life you will experience great joys as well as some very difficult times. Regardless of where you find yourself along the way, there is one thing that will never, ever change.

That one thing is the pleasure—the delight—of God for you. God created you according to His good pleasure. Nothing can take this away from you... because *it's His will*. As we conclude this book, let's look at this world's most compelling story.

> "Having predestined us to adoption... by Jesus Christ to Himself, *according to the good pleasure of His will,* to the praise of the glory of His grace, by which He made us accepted in the Beloved." Ephesians 1:5-6; NKJV, italics added

HIS STORY

The story of God all throughout history is one of love. *Everything* He does is motivated by love. When you come to a place where you believe God truly loves—and absolutely takes pleasure in you—you will be able to receive all that He has for you.

> "You, LORD, are forgiving and good,
> abounding in love to all who call to You...
> You, LORD, are a compassionate and gracious God,
> slow to anger, abounding in love and faithfulness."
> Psalm 86:5, 15; NIV

> "The LORD directs the steps of the godly.
> He delights in every detail of their lives.
> Though they stumble, they will never fall,
> for the LORD holds them by the hand." Psalm 37:23-24; NLT

> "For the LORD takes pleasure in His people..."
> Psalm 149:4a; NKJV

> "It is God who works in you both to will and to do for His good pleasure." Philippians 2:13; NKJV

His pleasure will change how you see yourself and everything around you. It will literally transform you as it brings great security to your life. But how do you access the reality of God's pleasure in the ups and downs of life? You believe it. Believe and step into His provision for you as you meditate on the Scripture below.

> "I pray that out of His glorious riches He may strengthen you with power through His Spirit in your inner being... that you being rooted and established in love... may be filled to the measure of all the fullness of God." Ephesians 3:16, 17b, 19b; NIV

Look at what God has personally given to you:
  • He strengthens you with His power.
  • He establishes you in His love.
  • He fills you with the fullness of Himself.

Why does He do this? So that you would know His great love for you. Everything He does declares His love. There is nothing missing or lacking in Him, and His provision is to give you all of Himself—His fullness. Because He loves you!

BE LOVED AND BE HELD

As you walk in the green pastures, through the valleys, and over the mountains of your life, God wants you to be sustained by His goodness and delight—by His love. You are the beloved of the Lord. He is fully committed to you, and He's given you everything you need to live in victory.

If you are tired and weary:
Let Him hold you!
Let Him comfort you!
Let Him pour His love upon you and encourage you!

"The LORD is near to those who have a broken heart,
And saves such as have a contrite spirit." Psalm 34:18; NKJV

"The LORD is good,
a refuge in times of trouble.
He cares for those who trust in Him." Nahum 1:7; NIV

"For the LORD your God is living among you.
He is a mighty savior.
He will take delight in you with gladness.
With His love, He will calm all your fears.
He will rejoice over you with joyful songs." Zephaniah 3:17; NLT

I pray with all my heart that as you've read through this book you have found valuable keys you can utilize that help you step into your own personal victory so you can succeed in all you do.

Message from God's Heart:

"I love you, My precious one.
    I love you.
    I love you.
    I love you.

The world will try to dilute this.
The enemy will try to make you doubt it.
Your circumstances will challenge it.

…But My love is the truest truth you can know!
It is the foundation of everything.
It's why I created you.
It's why I paid the highest price so you could freely come to Me and receive all that I am.

Here is a secret:
If you ever find yourself feeling tired and discouraged,
you have become disconnected from the lifeline of My love.
All you need to do is sit with Me and reconnect.

Remember who I am.
Remember what I've given.
And receive it.

Let Me love and hold you closely.
Let Me fill you anew.
Through My love you will find your greatest victory.

I bless you richly, My anointed, precious, overcoming one!

"And God is able to bless you abundantly,
so that in all things at all times,
having all that you need,
you will abound in every good work."

2 Corinthians 9:8; NIV

ABOUT THE AUTHOR

Diane Hunter, with her husband Roger, are the co-founders of Epic Life Ministries. Their mission is:

"Growing in the fullness of God...
Choosing life, freedom, and identity in Christ."

Please visit their website: www.epiclifeministries.com to get more information about the ministry, read Diane's blog, or to order books.

Diane is an ordained pastor, an author, and a broadcaster on the Holy Spirit Broadcasting Network:
http://hsbn.tv/broadcaster.html?b=E303DC
—where you can view her broadcasts under "Epic Life Ministries."

Check out her other books:

• *Purity by Design,*
https://www.epiclifeministries.com/
purity-by-design-book

• *Fulfilling your Destiny,*
https://www.epiclifeministries.com/
fulfilling-your-destiny-book

And, although Diane has a Masters of Divinity from Talbot School of Theology and has received an honorary Doctorate of Divinity from HSBN International Fellowship of Ministries, her main qualification and goal in ministry is loving God and loving His people. It's to usher people into all that God has so we can live in the fullness of His joy.

.

www.ingramcontent.com/pod-product-compliance
Lightning Source LLC
LaVergne TN
LVHW041323080426
835513LV00008B/574